Contents

Cambridge School Shakespeare

This edition of *As You Like It* is part of the *Cambridge School Shakespeare* series. Like every other play in the series, it has been specially prepared to help all students in schools and colleges.

This *As You Like It* aims to be different from other editions of the play. It invites you to bring the play to life in your classroom, hall or drama studio through enjoyable activities that will increase your understanding. Actors have created their different interpretations of the play over the centuries. Similarly, you are encouraged to make up your own mind about *As You Like It*, rather than having someone else's interpretation handed down to you.

Cambridge School Shakespeare does not offer you a cut-down or simplified version of the play. This is Shakespeare's language, filled with imaginative possibilities. You will find on every left-hand page: a summary of the action, an explanation of unfamiliar words, and a choice of activities on Shakespeare's language, characters and stories.

Between each act and in the pages at the end of the play, you will find notes, illustrations and activities. These will help to increase your understanding of the whole play.

There are a large number of activities to give you the widest choice to suit your own particular needs. Please don't think you have to do every one. Choose the activities that help you most.

This edition will be of value to you whether you are studying for an examination, reading for pleasure, or thinking of putting on the play to entertain others. You can work on the activities on your own or in groups. Many of the activities suggest a particular group size, but don't be afraid to make up smaller or larger groups to suit your own purposes.

Although you are invited to treat *As You Like It* as a play, you don't need special dramatic or theatrical skills to do the activities. By choosing your activities, and by exploring and experimenting, you can make your own interpretations of Shakespeare's language, characters and stories. Whatever you do, remember that Shakespeare wrote his plays to be acted, watched and enjoyed.

Rex Gibson

This edition of *As You Like It* uses the text of the play established by Michael Hattaway in *The New Cambridge Shakespeare*.

Shakespeare

As You Like It

Edited by Rex Gibson

Series Editor: Rex Gibson
Director, Shakespeare and Schools Project

PUBLISHED BY THE PRESS SYNDICATE OF THE UNIVERSITY OF CAMBRIDGE
The Pitt Building, Trumpington Street, Cambridge, United Kingdom

CAMBRIDGE UNIVERSITY PRESS
The Edinburgh Building, Cambridge CB2 2RU, UK http://www.cup.cam.ac.uk
40 West 20th Street, New York, NY 10011–4211, USA http://www.cup.org
10 Stamford Road, Oakleigh, Melbourne 3166, Australia
Ruiz de Alarcón 13, 28014 Madrid, Spain

First published 2000

Printed in the United Kingdom at the University Press, Cambridge

Typeface Monotype Ehrhardt 11/13pt *System* QuarkXPress™

A catalogue record for this book is available from the British Library

Library of Congress Cataloguing in Publication data applied for

ISBN 0 521 66636 8

Prepared for publication by Stenton Associates
Designed by Richard Morris, Stonesfield Design
Picture research by Callie Kendall

Thanks are due to the following for permission to reproduce photographs:
Cover: Globe Theatre, 1998, John Tramper; Samuel Palmer, *Pastoral Scene with Horse Chestnut Tree*, Ashmolean Museum, Oxford; 18 (RSC 1989), 26 (RSC 1977), 187 (RSC 1977), Joe Cocks Studio Collection, Shakespeare Centre Library; 33, 44, 52, 64, 109, 120, 133, 134, 142, 167, 171, 175, 185, Donald Cooper/Photostage; 68, Shakespeare Institute, University of Birmingham; 94 (RSC 1992), Alastair Muir; 114, 169, Zoe Dominic; 172 (SMT 1937), Shakespeare Centre Library

List of characters

The court

The usurping court

DUKE FREDERICK
CELIA his daughter (who disguises herself as Aliena)
ROSALIND daughter of Duke Senior (who disguises herself as Ganymede)
TOUCHSTONE a clown
CHARLES the duke's wrestler
LE BEAU, FIRST LORD, SECOND LORD — courtiers

The de Boys household

OLIVER, JAQUES, ORLANDO — sons of Sir Roland de Boys
ADAM servant to Orlando
DENIS servant to Oliver

The Forest of Arden

The banished court

DUKE SENIOR the rightful duke
JAQUES, AMIENS, FIRST LORD, SECOND LORD — courtiers
FIRST PAGE, SECOND PAGE — attendants on the duke

The people of Arden

CORIN a shepherd
SILVIUS a shepherd
PHEBE a shepherdess
AUDREY a goatherd
WILLIAM a countryman
SIR OLIVER MARTEXT a priest
FORESTERS

HYMEN god of marriage

The action of the play takes place in Oliver's home, Duke Frederick's palace and the Forest of Arden

Orlando recounts how he inherited only £250. His father's will instructed the oldest son, Oliver, to educate Orlando. But Oliver treats him worse than the horses, and denies him status or education.

---

1 Invent a scene (in groups of four)

In 1998, at Shakespeare's Globe Theatre on London's Bankside, the play began with a scene based on Orlando's first speech. It showed old Sir Roland de Boys making his will bequeathing the bulk of his estate to his oldest son, Oliver. He blessed Oliver and ordered him to educate the other two sons.

Jaques, the second son, went off to study at university, and the youngest son, Orlando, was given £250 ('but poor a thousand crowns'). It was clear that old Sir Roland expected Oliver to treat Orlando well. But Oliver showed the audience that he had no intention of carrying out his father's wishes. As soon as his father died, he began mistreating Orlando.

Stage your own scene in which Sir Roland de Boys, on his deathbed, tells his three sons what is in his will and what he wants them to do. In the Globe production, a singer sang a ballad describing the events. You may wish to write your own ballad to accompany a mime showing the father and three sons.

2 Speak Orlando's story (in pairs)

Take turns to explore different styles of speaking lines 1–19. Is Orlando bitter or merely sad as he complains about his brother?

3 Jaques de Boys

No more will be heard of the brother who is doing so well at university until the last scene in the play. You will discover (in Act 2) another Jaques who is a major character in *As You Like It*.

---

charged ordered
breed educate
rustically like a peasant
unkept uncared for, uneducated
stalling sheltering
manège paces, stylish behaviour
dearly hired paid well
countenance behaviour, attitude
hinds farm labourers
bars denies
mines my gentility undermines my nobility
mar spoil

As You Like It

Act 1 Scene 1
The orchard of Oliver's house

Enter ORLANDO and ADAM

ORLANDO As I remember, Adam, it was upon this fashion bequeathed me by will but poor a thousand crowns and, as thou say'st, charged my brother, on his blessing, to breed me well: and there begins my sadness. My brother Jaques he keeps at school, and report speaks goldenly of his profit. For my part, he keeps me rustically at home or, to speak more properly, stays me here at home unkept – for call you that 'keeping' for a gentleman of my birth, that differs not from the stalling of an ox? His horses are bred better for, besides that they are fair with their feeding, they are taught their manège, and to that end riders dearly hired. But I, his brother, gain nothing under him but growth – for the which his animals on his dunghills are as much bound to him as I. Besides this nothing that he so plentifully gives me, the something that Nature gave me his countenance seems to take from me: he lets me feed with his hinds, bars me the place of a brother, and, as much as in him lies, mines my gentility with my education. This is it, Adam, that grieves me, and the spirit of my father, which I think is within me, begins to mutiny against this servitude. I will no longer endure it, though yet I know no wise remedy how to avoid it.

Enter OLIVER

ADAM Yonder comes my master, your brother.

ORLANDO Go apart, Adam, and thou shalt hear how he will shake me up.

[*Adam withdraws*]

OLIVER Now sir, what make you here?

ORLANDO Nothing: I am not taught to make anything.

OLIVER What mar you then, sir?

Oliver is angered by Orlando's protest at being kept in poverty. He threatens to strike Orlando, but Orlando seizes Oliver and demands his share of the will. Oliver seems to consent.

---

1 Brother against brother (in groups of three)

Take parts as Orlando, Oliver and Adam (who can also act as director) to rehearse and stage lines 20–67. Use the following suggestions to help your presentation.

- The brothers call each other 'sir', but in what tones of voice?
- Orlando often echoes his brother's words. Emphasise all the repetitions to make them as insulting as possible.
- Orlando appeals to his brother as a born gentleman ('the gentle condition of blood') to treat him also as a gentleman. How can you show that both brothers are acutely conscious of their social status as the sons of a gentleman?

2 'What prodigal portion …?'

Orlando's lines 29–30 echo the parable of the Prodigal Son in the Bible (Luke 15.11–32), who wasted his inheritance and became so poor that he was forced to eat pigfood ('husks'). You will find other echoes of the Bible as you work through the play.

3 Staging the fight (in pairs)

Orlando is the younger brother, but he proves he is better at fighting than his brother ('you are too young in this'). The stage directions at lines 41, 42 and 59 were not written by Shakespeare, but inserted by the editor of this edition. They suggest that Oliver begins the physical violence – but does he? Work out how you would stage the fight in a way that reveals the personality of each brother.

Marry by the Virgin Mary
be naught awhile clear off!
penury poverty
courtesy of nations social custom
allows you my better says you are superior
is nearer to his reverence makes you his legitimate heir
villein serf, lowest-status person (pun on 'villain')
accord peace
allottery share, bequest
testament will

ORLANDO Marry, sir, I am helping you to mar that which God made, a poor unworthy brother of yours, with idleness.

OLIVER Marry, sir, be better employed, and be naught awhile.

ORLANDO Shall I keep your hogs and eat husks with them? What prodigal portion have I spent that I should come to such penury?

OLIVER Know you where you are, sir?

ORLANDO O, sir, very well: here in your orchard.

OLIVER Know you before whom, sir?

ORLANDO Aye, better than him I am before knows me: I know you are my eldest brother, and in the gentle condition of blood you should so know me. The courtesy of nations allows you my better in that you are the first-born, but the same tradition takes not away my blood, were there twenty brothers betwixt us. I have as much of my father in me as you, albeit I confess your coming before me is nearer to his reverence.

OLIVER [*Raising his hand*] What, boy!

ORLANDO [*Seizing his brother*] Come, come, elder brother, you are too young in this.

OLIVER Wilt thou lay hands on me, villain?

ORLANDO I am no villein: I am the youngest son of Sir Roland de Boys; he was my father, and he is thrice a villain that says such a father begot villeins. Wert thou not my brother, I would not take this hand from thy throat till this other had pulled out thy tongue for saying so: thou hast railed on thyself.

ADAM [*Coming forward*] Sweet masters, be patient, for your father's remembrance, be at accord.

OLIVER Let me go, I say.

ORLANDO I will not till I please. You shall hear me. My father charged you in his will to give me good education: you have trained me like a peasant, obscuring and hiding from me all gentleman-like qualities. The spirit of my father grows strong in me – and I will no longer endure it. Therefore allow me such exercises as may become a gentleman or give me the poor allottery my father left me by testament: with that I will go buy my fortunes.

[*He releases Oliver*]

OLIVER And what wilt thou do? Beg when that is spent? Well, sir, get you in. I will not long be troubled with you: you shall have some part of your 'will'; I pray you leave me.

Oliver resolves to get rid of Orlando. Charles tells of Duke Senior's banishment, Rosalind and Celia's great friendship, and of many courtiers joining Duke Senior in the Forest of Arden.

---

1 Oliver's soliloquies (in pairs)

Oliver shows the unpleasant side of his nature, calling the faithful servant Adam 'old dog'. He then has two short soliloquies, lines 68–9 and line 75. The stage convention is that in a soliloquy a character speaks the truth, and shows their true personality and intentions. Experiment with different deliveries of the soliloquies. For example, might Oliver pause menacingly before line 75, hinting that the wrestling might be a way of getting rid of his brother?

2 Setting the mood

Charles' news helps to establish the play's atmosphere and themes:

Quarrelling brothers: Duke Frederick has banished his brother, Duke Senior.

Female friendship: Rosalind and Celia, daughters of the hostile dukes, are inseparable friends.

The pastoral world: Duke Senior has gone into exile in the Forest of Arden (see pages 172–3). It is like 'the golden world' (line 95) of classical Greek and Latin mythology: an idyllic long-ago place where no one worked, but enjoyed themselves in poetry, song, dance and lovemaking. In English folklore, it was the world of Robin Hood: a famous outlaw who lived with his 'Merry Men' in Sherwood Forest in Nottinghamshire.

In one production, Oliver looked amazed as Charles spoke lines 92–5 with great lyricism. Charles also seemed surprised by his own eloquence. As he ended, he paused, then shrugged apologetically. Suggest why Shakespeare gave Charles such expressive language, and how he (a wrestler) might be dressed at this moment.

---

grow upon me become troublesome to me
physic your rankness cure your fast growing insolence
importunes begs
old duke Duke Senior
new duke Duke Frederick
good leave cheerful permission
the duke's daughter, her cousin Celia
fleet the time carelessly pass the time without a care

ORLANDO I will no further offend you than becomes me for my good.

OLIVER [*To Adam*] Get you with him, you old dog.

ADAM Is 'old dog' my reward? Most true, I have lost my teeth in your service. God be with my old master: he would not have spoke such a word.

Exeunt Orlando [*and*] *Adam*

OLIVER Is it even so, begin you to grow upon me? I will physic your rankness, and yet give no thousand crowns neither. – Holla, Denis.

Enter DENIS

DENIS Calls your worship?

OLIVER Was not Charles, the duke's wrestler, here to speak with me?

DENIS So please you, he is here at the door, and importunes access to you.

OLIVER Call him in.

[*Exit Denis*]

'Twill be a good way, and tomorrow the wrestling is.

Enter CHARLES

CHARLES Good morrow to your worship.

OLIVER Good Monsieur Charles, what's the new news at the new court?

CHARLES There's no news at the court, sir, but the old news: that is, the old duke is banished by his younger brother, the new duke, and three or four loving lords have put themselves into voluntary exile with him, whose lands and revenues enrich the new duke; therefore he gives them good leave to wander.

OLIVER Can you tell if Rosalind, the duke's daughter, be banished with her father?

CHARLES O no; for the duke's daughter, her cousin, so loves her, being ever from their cradles bred together, that she would have followed her exile or have died to stay behind her; she is at the court and no less beloved of her uncle than his own daughter, and never two ladies loved as they do.

OLIVER Where will the old duke live?

CHARLES They say he is already in the Forest of Arden, and a many merry men with him; and there they live like the old Robin Hood of England. They say many young gentlemen flock to him every day, and fleet the time carelessly as they did in the golden world.

Charles says he is reluctant to injure Orlando. Oliver falsely describes Orlando's character and intentions, and urges Charles to kill him. Alone on stage, Oliver expresses envy of Orlando's character and reputation.

1 Charles – what's he like?

Charles is the duke's wrestler. He is very proud of his reputation ('credit'), and warns of what may happen if Orlando insists on fighting him ('hath a disposition' = intends). Describe the kind of person you would cast to play the role. Advise him how to deliver lines 97–107 in ways that reveal his character.

2 A false brother (in pairs)

a One person speaks everything Oliver says in lines 108–23, pausing after every short section. In the pause, the other person says 'True' or 'False', to identify whether or not Oliver is lying.

b Oliver's descriptions of Orlando are often descriptions of himself (for example, 'envious emulator' = jealous imitator, 'villainous contriver' = wicked plotter). Psychoanalysts call this 'projection', that is, attributing your own feelings or characteristics to others. Make two lists, one headed 'Oliver', the other headed 'Orlando'. Work through the lines, writing each description under the appropriate name.

c After his false catalogue of Orlando's bad character, Oliver says 'I speak but brotherly of him' (line 121). Suggest how you would wish the audience to respond to that remark, and advise Oliver how to deliver it to achieve that response.

d Why does Oliver hate Orlando so much? Take turns to speak lines 127–34, then talk together about what motivates Oliver's hatred of his brother.

---

loath to foil reluctant to defeat
brook endure
own search own wishing
requite reward
underhand means secret methods
as lief as soon
anatomise him analyse his faults
stir this gamester shake this upstart
noble device nobility
all sorts everybody
altogether misprized scorned by everyone
kindle the boy encourage Orlando

OLIVER What, you wrestle tomorrow before the new duke?

CHARLES Marry, do I, sir; and I came to acquaint you with a matter. I am given, sir, secretly to understand that your younger brother Orlando hath a disposition to come in, disguised, against me to try a fall. Tomorrow, sir, I wrestle for my credit, and he that escapes me without some broken limb shall acquit him well. Your brother is but young and tender and, for your love, I would be loath to foil him, as I must for my own honour, if he come in; therefore, out of my love to you, I came hither to acquaint you withal, that either you might stay him from his intendment, or brook such disgrace well as he shall run into, in that it is a thing of his own search and altogether against my will.

OLIVER Charles, I thank thee for thy love to me, which thou shalt find I will most kindly requite. I had myself notice of my brother's purpose herein, and have by underhand means laboured to dissuade him from it – but he is resolute. I'll tell thee, Charles, it is the stubbornest young fellow of France, full of ambition, an envious emulator of every man's good parts, a secret and villainous contriver against me, his natural brother. Therefore use thy discretion: I had as lief thou didst break his neck as his finger. And thou wert best look to't – for if thou dost him any slight disgrace or if he do not mightily grace himself on thee, he will practise against thee by poison, entrap thee by some treacherous device, and never leave thee till he hath ta'en thy life by some indirect means or other. For I assure thee – and almost with tears I speak it – there is not one so young and so villainous this day living. I speak but brotherly of him, but should I anatomise him to thee as he is, I must blush and weep, and thou must look pale and wonder.

CHARLES I am heartily glad I came hither to you. If he come tomorrow, I'll give him his payment; if ever he go alone again, I'll never wrestle for prize more – and so God keep your worship. *Exit*

OLIVER Farewell, good Charles. – Now will I stir this gamester. I hope I shall see an end of him, for my soul – yet I know not why – hates nothing more than he. Yet he's gentle, never schooled and yet learned, full of noble device, of all sorts enchantingly beloved, and indeed so much in the heart of the world, and especially of my own people who best know him, that I am altogether misprized. But it shall not be so long this wrestler shall clear all: nothing remains but that I kindle the boy thither, which now I'll go about.

Exit

Celia tries to cheer Rosalind, who thinks with sadness of her banished father. Responding to Celia's affection, Rosalind joins in witty wordplay about love, fortune and nature.

---

1 'Devise sports' – let's talk! (in pairs)

Celia promises Rosalind that she will put right her father's wrong, by eventually giving back everything Duke Frederick has seized from Rosalind's father, Duke Senior. She manages to persuade Rosalind to be merry and the two women begin to 'devise sports': play games with language. Such language games were a familiar pastime among court ladies in Shakespeare's day. One lady would propose a topic, and everyone would try to outdo the others in witty wordplay on that subject.

Rosalind proposes they talk about falling in love. Celia says love is only worth joking about, and Rosalind should not love any man seriously ('in good earnest') or playfully ('in sport'), in ways that might cause shame (lines 21–3).

Celia then proposes her own topic: 'housewife Fortune' who turned a wheel, sending men and women at random to positions of wealth and power, or poverty and powerlessness. Rosalind replies that 'the bountiful blind woman' (fortune was often portrayed as a blindfolded goddess) is unfair to women. Celia agrees, saying beautiful women ('fair') are rarely virtuous ('honest'), and virtuous women look ugly ('ill-favouredly'). Rosalind challenges Celia, saying that fortune only affects things like wealth and power ('gifts of the world'), and that a person's looks, intelligence and moral qualities are given by nature ('the lineaments of Nature').

Today, actors playing Rosalind and Celia face the challenge of how to make their wordplay intelligible and amusing to a modern audience. Step into role as the characters. Speak lines 1–45, then talk together about how you would stage this episode.

---

coz cousin
still always
righteously tempered properly strengthened
condition of my estate my situation
perforce by force
render give back to
devise sports think up amusements
make sport withal joke about it
with safety … off again you can end without shame

ACT 1 SCENE 2
Duke Frederick's palace

Enter ROSALIND and CELIA

CELIA I pray thee, Rosalind, sweet my coz, be merry.

ROSALIND Dear Celia, I show more mirth than I am mistress of, and would you yet I were merrier: unless you could teach me to forget a banished father, you must not learn me how to remember any extraordinary pleasure.

CELIA Herein, I see, thou lov'st me not with the full weight that I love thee; if my uncle, thy banished father, had banished thy uncle, the duke my father, so thou hadst been still with me, I could have taught my love to take thy father for mine; so wouldst thou, if the truth of thy love to me were so righteously tempered as mine is to thee.

ROSALIND Well, I will forget the condition of my estate to rejoice in yours.

CELIA You know my father hath no child but I, nor none is like to have; and, truly, when he dies thou shalt be his heir: for what he hath taken away from thy father perforce I will render thee again in affection. By mine honour, I will, and when I break that oath, let me turn monster. Therefore, my sweet Rose, my dear Rose, be merry.

ROSALIND From henceforth I will, coz, and devise sports. Let me see, what think you of falling in love?

CELIA Marry, I prithee do, to make sport withal: but love no man in good earnest – nor no further in sport neither – than with safety of a pure blush thou mayst in honour come off again.

ROSALIND What shall be our sport then?

CELIA Let us sit and mock the good housewife Fortune from her wheel, that her gifts may henceforth be bestowed equally.

ROSALIND I would we could do so: for her benefits are mightily misplaced, and the bountiful blind woman doth most mistake in her gifts to women.

CELIA 'Tis true, for those that she makes fair she scarce makes honest, and those that she makes honest she makes very ill-favouredly.

ROSALIND Nay, now thou goest from Fortune's office to Nature's: Fortune reigns in gifts of the world, not in the lineaments of Nature.

Celia comments that fools are sent by nature to sharpen witty people's intelligence. Touchstone jokes about honour. He hints at corruption in Duke Frederick's court.

---

1 Social superiority?

Imagine you are directing the play. The actor playing Celia says to you 'I'm unhappy about speaking line 44 ("the dullness of the fool is the whetstone of the wits"). It's saying that it's acceptable for clever people to laugh at ordinary people'. What do you reply?

2 First sight of Touchstone (in groups of three)

Touchstone is Duke Frederick's jester or fool. Noblemen often kept such a person, whose role was to sing, joke and entertain in the household. Fools had licence to criticise the follies of their masters and other high-status people. But as Celia's line 67 shows, if a fool's criticism offended his master, he was whipped.

Like all Shakespeare's clowns, Touchstone loves playing with language, joking to make a serious point. His story of the knight and the pancakes (lines 50–65) may be a veiled criticism of Duke Frederick's court, implying it lacks honour.

Take parts and act lines 45–72 to bring out the comedy, especially where Touchstone tricks the two women into stroking their chins and swearing by their non-existent beards.

3 Comments on Shakespeare's times? (in small groups)

Lines 68–72 may be Shakespeare's comment on an act of censorship in 1599, when Queen Elizabeth I's government ordered the burning of satirical pamphlets. Another interpretation is that Shakespeare is satirising City of London officials ('wise men') who persecuted the actors ('fools'). Talk together about whether audiences today need these interpretations to help them enjoy the humour.

---

flout mock
Nature's natural idiot, born fool
Peradventure perhaps
to reason to talk about
whetstone sharpening stone
pancakes fritters, burgers
naught worthless
forsworn perjured, lying on oath
unmuzzle unleash, set free
Prithee I pray you (pardon)
taxation slander, criticism
troth faith

Enter TOUCHSTONE

CELIA No? When Nature hath made a fair creature, may she not by Fortune fall into the fire? Though Nature hath given us wit to flout at Fortune, hath not Fortune sent in this fool to cut off the argument?

ROSALIND Indeed there is Fortune too hard for Nature, when Fortune makes Nature's natural the cutter-off of Nature's wit.

CELIA Peradventure this is not Fortune's work neither but Nature's who, perceiving our natural wits too dull to reason of such goddesses, hath sent this natural for our whetstone: for always the dullness of the fool is the whetstone of the wits. – How now, wit, whither wander you?

TOUCHSTONE Mistress, you must come away to your father.

CELIA Were you made the messenger?

TOUCHSTONE No, by mine honour, but I was bid to come for you.

ROSALIND Where learned you that oath, fool?

TOUCHSTONE Of a certain knight that swore, by his honour, they were good pancakes, and swore, by his honour, the mustard was naught. Now, I'll stand to it, the pancakes were naught and the mustard was good – and yet was not the knight forsworn.

CELIA How prove you that in the great heap of your knowledge?

ROSALIND Aye, marry, now unmuzzle your wisdom.

TOUCHSTONE Stand you both forth now. Stroke your chins and swear, by your beards, that I am a knave.

CELIA By our beards – if we had them – thou art.

TOUCHSTONE By my knavery – if I had it – then I were. But if you swear by that that is not you are not forsworn: no more was this knight swearing by his honour, for he never had any; or if he had, he had sworn it away before ever he saw those pancakes or that mustard.

CELIA Prithee, who is't that thou mean'st?

TOUCHSTONE One that old Frederick, your father, loves.

CELIA My father's love is enough to honour him. Enough! Speak no more of him; you'll be whipped for taxation one of these days.

TOUCHSTONE The more pity that fools may not speak wisely what wise men do foolishly.

CELIA By my troth, thou say'st true: for, since the little wit that fools have was silenced, the little foolery that wise men have makes a great show. – Here comes 'Monsieur the Beau'.

Celia, Rosalind and Touchstone all mock Le Beau for his affected speech. He brings news of how Charles has seriously injured an old man's three sons. The news dismays the women.

1 Mocking Le Beau (in groups of four)

Le Beau is French for 'the beautiful'. He is often played as an over-dressed courtier who puts on airs and graces, using elaborate gestures and speaking with an affected accent (pronouncing 'sport' as 'spot'). On stage, he usually fails to see that Celia, Rosalind and Touchstone are mocking him. Consider each of the following to help your playing of lines 73–116.

Line 76: '*Bonjour*' – why and how might Celia speak in French?

Line 79 : 'Sport' – how does Celia imitate Le Beau?

Lines 81–2: Rosalind and Touchstone use pompously exaggerated language.

Line 83: Celia uses an image from bricklaying, suggesting that Touchstone is thickly laying on the irony, like a bricklayer slapping on a trowelful of mortar. Does Le Beau overhear her?

Line 94 and lines 96–7: How does Le Beau react to these interruptions? (Rosalind puns on Le Beau's use of 'presence'. Bills were legal documents which often began 'Be it known unto all men by these presents'.)

2 Cruelty at court

Charles the wrestler has nearly killed the three sons of an old man. Le Beau calls this 'sport', but Touchstone ironically reveals its cruel nature. Give your reply to the student who wrote about lines 108–9: 'But today many women enjoy watching wrestling. In Shakespeare's day, women watched much crueller "sports", like bear-baiting.'

---

put on us force-feed us with
marketable valuable, saleable (because heavier)
colour kind, nature
destinies decree goddesses of fate enforce
rank status (Rosalind replies with a pun on 'rank' meaning stinking)
dole sad weeping
beholders spectators

Enter LE BEAU

ROSALIND With his mouth full of news.

CELIA Which he will put on us as pigeons feed their young.

ROSALIND Then shall we be news-crammed.

CELIA All the better: we shall be the more marketable. – *Bonjour*, Monsieur Le Beau, what's the news?

LE BEAU Fair princess, you have lost much good sport.

CELIA 'Sport': of what colour?

LE BEAU 'What colour', madam? How shall I answer you?

ROSALIND As wit and fortune will.

TOUCHSTONE [*Imitating Le Beau*] Or as the destinies decree.

CELIA Well said: that was laid on with a trowel.

TOUCHSTONE Nay, if I keep not my rank –

ROSALIND Thou loosest thy old smell.

LE BEAU You amaze me, ladies! I would have told you of good wrestling which you have lost the sight of.

ROSALIND Yet tell us the manner of the wrestling.

LE BEAU I will tell you the beginning and, if it please your ladyships, you may see the end, for the best is yet to do; and here where you are they are coming to perform it.

CELIA Well, the beginning that is dead and buried.

LE BEAU There comes an old man and his three sons –

CELIA I could match this beginning with an old tale.

LE BEAU Three proper young men, of excellent growth and presence –

ROSALIND With bills on their necks: 'Be it known unto all men by these presents'.

LE BEAU The eldest of the three wrestled with Charles, the duke's wrestler, which Charles in a moment threw him and broke three of his ribs that there is little hope of life in him. So he served the second and so the third: yonder they lie, the poor old man, their father, making such pitiful dole over them that all the beholders take his part with weeping.

ROSALIND Alas.

TOUCHSTONE But what is the sport, monsieur, that the ladies have lost?

LE BEAU Why, this that I speak of.

TOUCHSTONE Thus men may grow wiser every day. It is the first time that ever I heard breaking of ribs was sport for ladies.

CELIA Or I, I promise thee.

The court and the wrestlers enter. Duke Frederick says Orlando insists on fighting, but Charles is certain to win the wrestling match. Celia and Rosalind try to persuade Orlando not to fight.

---

1 'Is yonder the man?'

This is the first time that Rosalind has set eyes on Orlando. Is it love at first sight? Advise Rosalind how to speak line 119.

2 Young Orlando

Count the number of times that Orlando's youthfulness is mentioned on the page opposite ('youth', 'too young', and so on). Suggest why Shakespeare emphasises Orlando's age at this moment.

3 Friendly or menacing or …?

Duke Frederick greets Celia ('daughter'), then Rosalind ('cousin'). Rosalind is actually his niece, but in Shakespeare's time 'cousin' was used much more freely and loosely than today. But in what tone of voice does Frederick say '– and cousin'? Remember he has banished Rosalind's father and seized his dukedom. Also consider why and how Frederick speaks 'crept' in line 122.

4 Show how they feel (in groups of three)

Duke Frederick thinks there is an overwhelming certainty that Charles will win ('such odds in the man'). Rosalind and Celia try unsuccessfully to persuade Orlando not to fight, telling him his honour will not be devalued ('reputation shall not therefore be misprized'). Realising he is determined, they give him their support. Speak lines 133–56 to show how each woman feels about Orlando.

---

any else longs anyone who wishes
broken music in his sides fracturing of bones (like a smashed violin)
dotes upon foolishly loves
Flourish fanfare of trumpets
entreated persuaded
forwardness rash bravery
successfully as if he might win
liege lord
fain gladly
is the general challenger offers to fight anybody
suit plea, request

ROSALIND But is there any else longs to see this broken music in his sides? Is there yet another dotes upon rib-breaking? Shall we see this wrestling, cousin?

LE BEAU You must if you stay here, for here is the place appointed for the wrestling and they are ready to perform it.

CELIA Yonder, sure, they are coming. Let us now stay and see it.

Flourish. Enter DUKE FREDERICK, LORDS, ORLANDO, CHARLES, *and* ATTENDANTS

DUKE FREDERICK Come on, since the youth will not be entreated, his own peril on his forwardness.

ROSALIND Is yonder the man?

LE BEAU Even he, madam.

ROSALIND Alas, he is too young; yet he looks successfully.

DUKE FREDERICK How now, daughter – and cousin: are you crept hither to see the wrestling?

ROSALIND Aye, my liege, so please you give us leave.

DUKE FREDERICK You will take little delight in it, I can tell you: there is such odds in the man. In pity of the challenger's youth, I would fain dissuade him, but he will not be entreated. Speak to him, ladies: see if you can move him.

CELIA Call him hither, good Monsieur Le Beau.

DUKE FREDERICK Do so; I'll not be by.

[*The Duke stands aside*]

LE BEAU Monsieur the challenger, the princess calls for you.

ORLANDO I attend them with all respect and duty.

ROSALIND Young man, have you challenged Charles the wrestler?

ORLANDO No, fair princess, he is the general challenger. I come but in as others do to try with him the strength of my youth.

CELIA Young gentleman, your spirits are too bold for your years: you have seen cruel proof of this man's strength. If you saw yourself with your eyes or knew yourself with your judgement, the fear of your adventure would counsel you to a more equal enterprise. We pray you, for your own sake, to embrace your own safety and give over this attempt.

ROSALIND Do, young sir: your reputation shall not therefore be misprized. We will make it our suit to the duke that the wrestling might not go forward.

Orlando says that he will lose nothing if he is defeated, because he is naturally unlucky and of no importance. Charles mocks him, but Rosalind and Celia support him. He defeats Charles.

The wrestling match. In a different production at the rebuilt Globe Theatre in London, the wrestling lasted several minutes, and took place all around the yard, among the audience. Work out your own staging of lines 157–73 to show how Orlando manages to beat the physically superior Charles.

hard thoughts strict judgement
trial test of strength
foiled defeated
gracious lucky, fortunate
supplied occupied
eke out add to
more modest working less ambitious aim
mightily persuaded see line 127 (is Charles mocking Duke Frederick?)
Hercules in Greek mythology, the world's strongest man
not yet well breathed barely warmed up

ORLANDO I beseech you, punish me not with your hard thoughts, wherein I confess me much guilty to deny so fair and excellent ladies anything. But let your fair eyes and gentle wishes go with me to my trial, wherein if I be foiled, there is but one shamed that was never gracious; if killed, but one dead that is willing to be so. I shall do my friends no wrong, for I have none to lament me; the world no injury, for in it I have nothing; only in the world I fill up a place, which may be better supplied when I have made it empty.

ROSALIND The little strength that I have, I would it were with you.

CELIA And mine to eke out hers.

ROSALIND Fare you well: pray heaven I be deceived in you.

CELIA Your heart's desires be with you.

CHARLES Come, where is this young gallant that is so desirous to lie with his mother earth?

ORLANDO Ready, sir, but his will hath in it a more modest working.

DUKE FREDERICK You shall try but one fall.

CHARLES No, I warrant your grace you shall not entreat him to a second, that have so mightily persuaded him from a first.

ORLANDO You mean to mock me after: you should not have mocked me before. But come your ways.

ROSALIND Now Hercules be thy speed, young man.

CELIA I would I were invisible, to catch the strong fellow by the leg.

[*They*] *wrestle*

ROSALIND O excellent young man.

CELIA If I had a thunderbolt in mine eye, I can tell who should down.

[*Charles is thrown to the ground.*] *Shout*

DUKE FREDERICK No more, no more.

ORLANDO Yes, I beseech your grace, I am not yet well breathed.

DUKE FREDERICK How dost thou, Charles?

LE BEAU He cannot speak, my lord.

DUKE FREDERICK Bear him away.

[*Charles is carried out*]

What is thy name, young man?

ORLANDO Orlando, my liege, the youngest son of Sir Roland de Boys.

Duke Frederick is displeased to find that Orlando is the son of his old enemy. Rosalind and Celia offer comfort to Orlando, but he seems unable to reply.

---

1 From prose to verse

Up to line 176 the characters have used prose. Now, for the first time in the play, they speak in verse. Perhaps Shakespeare switches from prose to verse because of the 'serious' nature of the duke's words. As you read on, think about why Shakespeare uses verse or prose for particular episodes. You can find help on page 178.

2 Why does Frederick hate old Sir Roland?

Duke Frederick (line 177) and Rosalind (lines 187–8) tell how Sir Roland de Boys was respected and honoured by everyone. Only Frederick saw him as an enemy. Suggest why Shakespeare makes Duke Frederick hostile to Orlando's much-loved father.

3 Stage business (in small groups)

Lines 184–6: To whom does Orlando speak – the departing court? the audience? the ladies?

Line 198: 'Wear this for me'. How does Rosalind hand over her chain, and how does Orlando receive it?

Line 204: 'He calls us back.' This line often evokes audience laughter because Orlando has not called them back, but Rosalind longs to speak to him again.

Lines 206–7: 'overthrown/More than your enemies.' How long do they '*gaze upon each other*' before Celia calls Rosalind away?

Line 208: 'Have with you' means 'I'm coming' or 'Hold on a minute'. How does Rosalind break her eye contact with Orlando?

---

still always
house family
calling name, birthright
given him tears unto entreaties added weeping to my pleas
Ere before
Sticks me at heart deeply pains me
mistress future wife
out of suits out of favour
better parts most human qualities
quintain wooden post (struck with lances by knights on horseback)

DUKE FREDERICK I would thou hadst been son to some man else;
The world esteemed thy father honourable
But I did find him still mine enemy.
Thou shouldst have better pleased me with this deed
Hadst thou descended from another house.
But fare thee well. Thou art a gallant youth:
I would thou hadst told me of another father.
[*Exeunt Duke Frederick, Le Beau, Touchstone, Lords, and Attendants*]
CELIA Were I my father, coz, would I do this?
ORLANDO I am more proud to be Sir Roland's son –
His youngest son – and would not change that calling
To be adopted heir to Frederick.
ROSALIND My father loved Sir Roland as his soul
And all the world was of my father's mind;
Had I before known this young man his son,
I should have given him tears unto entreaties
Ere he should thus have ventured.
CELIA Gentle cousin,
Let us go thank him and encourage him;
My father's rough and envious disposition
Sticks me at heart. – Sir, you have well deserved:
If you do keep your promises in love
But justly, as you have exceeded all promise,
Your mistress shall be happy.
ROSALIND [*Giving him a chain from her neck*] Gentleman,
Wear this for me: one out of suits with Fortune,
That could give more, but that her hand lacks means. –
Shall we go, coz?
CELIA Aye. – Fare you well, fair gentleman.
[*They turn to go*]
ORLANDO [*Aside*] Can I not say, 'I thank you'? My better parts
Are all thrown down, and that which here stands up
Is but a quintain, a mere lifeless block.
ROSALIND [*To Celia*] He calls us back. My pride fell with my fortunes,
I'll ask him what he would. – Did you call, sir?
Sir, you have wrestled well and overthrown
More than your enemies.
[*They gaze upon each other*]
CELIA Will you go, coz?
ROSALIND Have with you. – Fare you well.

Exeunt [*Rosalind and Celia*]

Orlando suspects he has fallen in love with Rosalind. Le Beau urges him to leave the court and so avoid Duke Frederick's malice, which is also directed at Rosalind.

---

1 'The duke is humorous'

Today, to say someone is 'humorous' means that they are amusing, with a lively sense of humour. But in Shakespeare's day it meant moody, unbalanced, unpredictable. That is because Elizabethans believed that a person's nature was governed by four 'humours', which, if they were not properly balanced, resulted in mood swings and extremes of anger, melancholy, bravery or calmness. You can find more about humours on page 132.

2 How would you play Le Beau?

In his earlier appearance, Le Beau seemed shallow and foppish. Now he offers good advice to Orlando as a friend. Step into role and speak his lines. Is he fearful of telling Orlando what he thinks Duke Frederick is really like (line 219)? At line 223, how might he convey his distaste for Duke Frederick's manners?

3 Did Shakespeare forget?

Le Beau says that Celia is taller than Rosalind. But you will shortly discover (Scene 3, line 105) that Rosalind is the taller of the two women. If you were acting Le Beau, would you change 'taller' to 'shorter' at line 224? Give reasons for your decision.

4 Disliking Rosalind, disliking Orlando (in pairs)

Compare lines 229–33 with how Oliver explains his hatred for Orlando in Scene 1, lines 128–32. What similarities can you find?

---

urged conference wished us to talk
Or Charles or if not Charles, **something weaker** (Rosalind)
Albeit although
misconsters misconstrues (misinterprets)
More suits you to conceive is better for you to imagine
ta'en displeasure 'gainst taken a dislike to
Grounded based
much bounden greatly indebted
from the smoke into the smother out of the frying pan into the fire

ORLANDO What passion hangs these weights upon my tongue?
I cannot speak to her, yet she urged conference.

Enter LE BEAU

O poor Orlando! thou art overthrown:
Or Charles or something weaker masters thee.

LE BEAU Good sir, I do in friendship counsel you
To leave this place. Albeit you have deserved
High commendation, true applause, and love,
Yet such is now the duke's condition
That he misconsters all that you have done.
The duke is humorous: what he is indeed
More suits you to conceive than I to speak of.

ORLANDO I thank you, sir; and pray you tell me this:
Which of the two was daughter of the duke,
That here was at the wrestling?

LE BEAU Neither his daughter, if we judge by manners,
But yet indeed the taller is his daughter;
The other is daughter to the banished duke
And here detained by her usurping uncle
To keep his daughter company, whose loves
Are dearer than the natural bond of sisters.
But I can tell you that of late this duke
Hath ta'en displeasure 'gainst his gentle niece,
Grounded upon no other argument
But that the people praise her for her virtues
And pity her for her good father's sake;
And, on my life, his malice 'gainst the lady
Will suddenly break forth. Sir, fare you well,
Hereafter, in a better world than this,
I shall desire more love and knowledge of you.

ORLANDO I rest much bounden to you: fare you well.

[*Exit Le Beau*]

Thus must I from the smoke into the smother,
From tyrant duke unto a tyrant brother.
But heavenly Rosalind! *Exit*

Celia tries to cheer Rosalind who seems downcast and love-sick for Orlando. She asks if Rosalind really has fallen in love so quickly, and jokes at her evasive reply. Duke Frederick enters, angry.

1 Cheering up Rosalind (in pairs)

The opening of Scene 3, with Rosalind seemingly disconsolate, contrasts sharply with the end of Scene 2, where Orlando is full of elation. Both moods spring from the same cause: falling in love. Take parts and work out how to stage lines 1–30, using the following to help you:

a Suggest how Celia and Rosalind enter to contrast with Orlando's exit, and what Rosalind might wear or carry to indicate her mood.

b How serious is Rosalind's dejection? Are her replies to Celia spoken in genuine sadness, or are they light-hearted responses, amusing both Celia and the audience? Or …?

c Celia tries to laugh Rosalind out of her unhappy mood, but at line 19 she abandons humour ('turning these jests out of service') and begins to talk seriously ('in good earnest'). Just how serious does she become? Decide whether lines 23–5 are a rebuke, or if they are laughingly spoken.

d Line 8 ('my child's father') shows that Rosalind is already thinking of Orlando as her husband. In Victorian times, many people thought the line too indecent for a young lady to say, so it was altered to 'my father's child' (Rosalind herself). Suggest ways in which Rosalind could speak both versions, and how Celia might react to each.

Cupid in Roman mythology, the god of love
laid up made ill
briars thorny branches, difficulties
burs prickly seed heads
holy-day foolery holiday play, fun
walk not in the trodden paths misbehave (stray from conventional ways)
Hem cough (or sew them up like the hem on a dress)
turning … service leaving this joking

Act I Scene 3
A room in Duke Frederick's palace

Enter CELIA and ROSALIND

CELIA Why cousin, why Rosalind – Cupid have mercy, not a word?

ROSALIND Not one to throw at a dog.

CELIA No, thy words are too precious to be cast away upon curs: throw some of them at me. Come, lame me with reasons.

ROSALIND Then there were two cousins laid up, when the one should be lamed with reasons, and the other mad without any.

CELIA But is all this for your father?

ROSALIND No, some of it is for my child's father – O how full of briars is this working-day world!

CELIA They are but burs, cousin, thrown upon thee in holy-day foolery: if we walk not in the trodden paths, our very petticoats will catch them.

ROSALIND I could shake them off my coat: these burs are in my heart.

CELIA Hem them away.

ROSALIND I would try, if I could cry 'hem' and have him.

CELIA Come, come, wrestle with thy affections.

ROSALIND O they take the part of a better wrestler than myself.

CELIA O, a good wish upon you: you will try in time in despite of a fall. But turning these jests out of service, let us talk in good earnest. Is it possible, on such a sudden, you should fall into so strong a liking with old Sir Roland's youngest son?

ROSALIND The duke my father loved his father dearly.

CELIA Doth it therefore ensue that you should love his son dearly? By this kind of chase I should hate him for my father hated his father dearly; yet I hate not Orlando.

ROSALIND No, faith, hate him not, for my sake.

CELIA Why should I not? Doth he not deserve well?

Enter DUKE FREDERICK *with* LORDS

ROSALIND Let me love him for that, and do you love him because I do. Look, here comes the duke.

CELIA With his eyes full of anger.

Duke Frederick banishes Rosalind on pain of death. She protests that neither she nor her father is a traitor. Celia supports her, saying she and Rosalind have been inseparable friends.

1 Banishment or death (in small groups)

Le Beau had earlier called Frederick 'humorous'. Here his moodiness and malice is seen in the two 'reasons' he gives for banishing Rosalind:

Line 45: 'Let it suffice thee that I trust thee not';

Line 48: 'Thou art thy father's daughter, there's enough'.

Talk together about how Rosalind reacts to her banishment and the death threat. Suggest how she delivers each of her responses to the duke. There are further activities on this episode on page 28.

Standing up to tyranny. Celia defies her father.
Choose a suitable caption to this picture from lines 56–79.

dispatch you … haste go immediately for your own safety
If with … hold intelligence if I understand myself
in a thought unborn subconsciously
purgation purification
grace itself virtue, goodness
mistake me not don't misjudge me
stayed her let her stay
ranged along also been banished
Juno's swans in Roman mythology, the swans drawing the chariot of the queen of the gods

DUKE FREDERICK Mistress, dispatch you with your safest haste
And get you from our court.
ROSALIND Me, uncle?
FREDERICK You, cousin.
Within these ten days if that thou be'st found
So near our public court as twenty miles,
Thou diest for it.
ROSALIND I do beseech your grace
Let me the knowledge of my fault bear with me:
If with myself I hold intelligence,
Or have acquaintance with mine own desires,
If that I do not dream or be not frantic
(As I do trust I am not) then, dear uncle,
Never so much as in a thought unborn,
Did I offend your highness.
DUKE FREDERICK Thus do all traitors:
If their purgation did consist in words,
They are as innocent as grace itself.
Let it suffice thee that I trust thee not.
ROSALIND Yet your mistrust cannot make me a traitor;
Tell me whereon the likelihoods depends?
DUKE FREDERICK Thou art thy father's daughter, there's enough.
ROSALIND So was I when your highness took his dukedom,
So was I when your highness banished him;
Treason is not inherited, my lord,
Or if we did derive it from our friends,
What's that to me? My father was no traitor.
Then, good my liege, mistake me not so much
To think my poverty is treacherous.
CELIA Dear sovereign, hear me speak.
DUKE FREDERICK Aye, Celia, we stayed her for your sake,
Else had she with her father ranged along.
CELIA I did not then entreat to have her stay,
It was your pleasure – and your own remorse.
I was too young that time to value her
But now I know her: if she be a traitor,
Why so am I. We still have slept together,
Rose at an instant, learned, played, eat together,
And wheresoe'er we went, like Juno's swans,
Still we went coupled and inseparable.

Duke Frederick rebukes Celia, saying Rosalind steals her good reputation. He again banishes Rosalind with threats of death. Celia proposes that she and Rosalind go to the Forest of Arden.

---

1 Banishment or death (in small groups)

a Talk together about how Duke Frederick's language and behaviour resembles that of Oliver's jealousy of Orlando.

b Is Frederick's sentencing of Rosalind done in angry haste, or in dignified, elaborate ceremony? How might you best portray on stage Duke Frederick's irrationality and inflexibility?

c Suggest how the lords attending on Duke Frederick behave as they watch and hear his angry words to his daughter and his niece.

d For an activity on fathers angrily rebuking their daughters in other plays by Shakespeare, see page 32.

e What do you feel is the most appropriate style for the duke and the lords to leave the stage?

2 Celia takes the lead

After standing up to her father, Celia takes the initiative in proposing a plan of escape. She declares that in banishing Rosalind, her father has banished her too. She says she will share Rosalind's changed fortune ('your change'), and swears by heaven, saying that it looks pale at their sadness (line 94), and that she will leave the court with Rosalind.

Does Celia reply immediately to Rosalind's question ('whither shall we go?'), or does she pause before deciding on the Forest of Arden? Experiment with both possibilities to find which you feel is most dramatically effective.

---

subtle crafty, cunning
name reputation
doom sentence, judgement
provide yourself prepare to leave
sundered separated
devise … fly plan together our escape

DUKE FREDERICK She is too subtle for thee, and her smoothness,
Her very silence, and her patience
Speak to the people and they pity her.
Thou art a fool: she robs thee of thy name
And thou wilt show more bright and seem more virtuous
When she is gone.

[*Celia starts to speak*]

Then open not thy lips!
Firm and irrevocable is my doom
Which I have passed upon her: she is banished.
CELIA Pronounce that sentence then on me, my liege,
I cannot live out of her company.
DUKE FREDERICK You are a fool. – You, niece, provide yourself:
If you outstay the time, upon mine honour
And in the greatness of my word, you die.

Exeunt Duke and Lords

CELIA O my poor Rosalind, whither wilt thou go?
Wilt thou change fathers? I will give thee mine!
I charge thee be not thou more grieved than I am.
ROSALIND I have more cause.
CELIA Thou hast not, cousin:
Prithee be cheerful. Know'st thou not the duke
Hath banished me, his daughter?
ROSALIND That he hath not.
CELIA No? 'Hath not'? Rosalind lacks then the love
Which teacheth thee that thou and I am one;
Shall we be sundered, shall we part, sweet girlie?
No, let my father seek another heir!
Therefore devise with me how we may fly,
Whither to go, and what to bear with us;
And do not seek to take your change upon you,
To bear your griefs yourself and leave me out:
For, by this heaven, now at our sorrows pale,
Say what thou canst, I'll go along with thee.
ROSALIND Why, whither shall we go?
CELIA To seek my uncle in the Forest of Arden.
ROSALIND Alas, what danger will it be to us
(Maids as we are) to travel forth so far?
Beauty provoketh thieves sooner than gold.

To avoid harassment, Celia proposes to disguise herself as a country girl. Rosalind decides to dress as a young man. They plan to take Touchstone with them to the Forest of Arden.

---

1 Contemporary references

Rosalind's plan to disguise herself as a boy will result in all kinds of comic ambiguities in the Forest of Arden. Shakespeare's Elizabethan audiences probably knew things about the lines opposite that are not common knowledge today:

- In Greek mythology, Ganymede was a beautiful young man. Jupiter (Jove), king of the gods, fell in love with him and, disguised as an eagle, seized and carried him off to Mount Olympus to become his cup-bearer ('page'). 'Ganymede' was also Elizabethan slang for a young male homosexual.
- Aliena is Latin for 'the stranger'. Celia's plan to rub earth or brown colouring ('umber') on her face recalls that in Shakespeare's time, court ladies took pride in their pale complexions. They considered suntanned women to be of lower social class (working in the open air).
- Lines 111–12 ('mannish cowards') may be Shakespeare's comment on the many boastful frauds who frequented London taverns. They had a swaggering, warlike appearance ('swashing and a martial outside'), and used it as a bluff ('outface') to sell false stories of their courage.

2 Three episodes, three moods (in small groups)

There are three distinct episodes in Scene 3: Rosalind's downcast mood; Duke Frederick's anger; and the excited planning of the escape to the Forest of Arden. Identify the lines for each sequence, and plan how to play the whole scene to bring out the changes of mood of each section.

---

mean attire unattractive dress
smirch make dirty
never stir assailants avoid harassment
common tall (see page 22, activity 3)
suit me all points dress entirely
curtal-axe cutlass, short broadsword
semblances outward appearances
assayed attempted
The clownish fool Touchstone
travail hardships, travel
woo persuade

CELIA I'll put myself in poor and mean attire
And with a kind of umber smirch my face;
The like do you. So shall we pass along
And never stir assailants.
ROSALIND Were it not better,
Because that I am more than common tall,
That I did suit me all points like a man,
A gallant curtal-axe upon my thigh,
A boar-spear in my hand, and in my heart
Lie there what hidden woman's fear there will.
We'll have a swashing and a martial outside
As many other mannish cowards have
That do outface it with their semblances.
CELIA What shall I call thee when thou art a man?
ROSALIND I'll have no worse a name than Jove's own page,
And therefore look you call me 'Ganymede'.
But what will you be called?
CELIA Something that hath a reference to my state:
No longer 'Celia', but 'Aliena'.
ROSALIND But, cousin, what if we assayed to steal
The clownish fool out of your father's court:
Would he not be a comfort to our travail?
CELIA He'll go along o'er the wide world with me:
Leave me alone to woo him. Let's away
And get our jewels and our wealth together,
Devise the fittest time and safest way
To hide us from pursuit that will be made
After my flight. Now go we in content,
To liberty, and not to banishment.

Exeunt

Looking back at Act 1

Activities for groups or individuals

1 Dramatic contrasts

Act 1 portrays some of the many juxtapositions in the play, as Shakespeare sets one feature against another: brother versus brother, male hostility versus female friendship, fortune versus nature, good versus evil, court versus forest. Step into role as director of the play and work out how you could emphasise one or more of the contrasts in the Act using sound effects, lighting, movement, costume, and so on.

2 A one-minute mime

Act 1 is full of lively and exciting action: the clash of brothers, a murderous plot, the wrestling match, love at first sight, the duke's anger, the death threat against Rosalind and her banishment, and the planned flight. Prepare a one-minute mime that portrays as vividly as possible the events of the Act.

3 What acting style?

The improbable events listed in activity 2 above set every new production of the play the problem of acting style. Should you play it naturalistically (as if it were real life), or like a fairy-tale, an obviously fictional world? Work in pairs as directors with very different views on the acting style suitable to the play. Argue your case (page 186 can help you).

4 Fathers and daughters

Duke Frederick angrily rebukes his daughter Celia, twice calling her a fool. Here is a list of daughters in other Shakespeare plays who at some time experience the displeasure of their fathers: Ophelia, Cordelia, Hero, Juliet, Imogen, Desdemona, Miranda, Hermia, Jessica, Sylvia. Identify the plays in which they appear. If you have to choose a research topic on *As You Like It*, you could compare the fathers and daughters in this play with those in several other plays.

5 Professor Profundo explains

Imagine you are Professor Profundo who thinks that every moment in every Shakespeare play is full of deep symbolic significance. Deliver your learned lecture on the 'true meaning of the wrestling match' in which your least controversial theory is that it portrays the power of love to conquer all. Let your imagination flow as wildly as you like.

In this open air production, Le Beau (right) tells the news of the wrestling to Rosalind, Celia and Touchstone. Compare the costumes here with those in other illustrations.

Duke Senior claims that life in the forest is far superior to life at court. Even its hardships are beneficial, and moral lessons are everywhere. He regrets that the deer are hunted and killed.

---

1 First sight of Arden (in pairs)

This is the first scene set in the Forest of Arden. Use the duke's first speech to suggest what the forest is like (you may change your first impression as you read on). Is it a warm and welcoming place, or is it cold, harsh and threatening? There may be clues in the duke's talk of 'the winter's wind', and of 'the penalty of Adam,/The seasons' difference' (lines 5–7). In the Bible, Adam, the first man, was driven out of Eden, a place of perpetual summer, into a world of changing seasons.

2 'Sweet are the uses of adversity' (in small groups)

The duke claims that misfortunes ('adversity') are valuable, that good can come out of afflictions. He uses an image from an old myth: the ugly toad that has a precious jewel in its head. Do you believe that troubles and hard knocks are good for you? Talk together about what you think of the duke's claim, using practical examples from your own experience.

3 Learning from nature (in pairs)

Lines 15–17 express the belief that human beings can learn from nature: that there are moral lessons in the landscape itself ('Sermons in stones'). William Wordsworth and his fellow Romantic poets held the same view two hundred years after Shakespeare (see page 69, activity 3). But does the duke speak with utter conviction of the truth of what he is saying, or is he just cheering himself up, or fooling himself, or …? Take turns to speak the lines in different styles.

---

co-mates companions
old custom long practice
painted pomp false ceremony of the court
churlish chiding harsh lashing
exempt from public haunt not visited by people
venison deer
irks troubles, distresses
dappled fools spotted creatures
native burghers born as citizens
desert city remote place
confines boundaries, territory
forkèd heads arrows
gored pierced, made bloody

Act 2 Scene 1
The Forest of Arden

Enter DUKE SENIOR, AMIENS, and two or three Lords dressed as foresters

DUKE SENIOR Now, my co-mates and brothers in exile,
Hath not old custom made this life more sweet
Than that of painted pomp? Are not these woods
More free from peril than the envious court?
Here feel we not the penalty of Adam,
The seasons' difference, as the icy fang
And churlish chiding of the winter's wind –
Which when it bites and blows upon my body
Even till I shrink with cold, I smile and say,
'This is no flattery' – these are counsellors
That feelingly persuade me what I am.
Sweet are the uses of adversity
Which like the toad, ugly and venomous,
Wears yet a precious jewel in his head,
And this our life exempt from public haunt
Finds tongues in trees, books in the running brooks,
Sermons in stones, and good in everything.
AMIENS I would not change it; happy is your grace
That can translate the stubbornness of fortune
Into so quiet and so sweet a style.
DUKE SENIOR Come, shall we go and kill us venison?
And yet it irks me the poor dappled fools,
Being native burghers of this desert city,
Should, in their own confines, with forkèd heads
Have their round haunches gored.
FIRST LORD Indeed, my lord.
The melancholy 'Jaques' grieves at that,
And in that kind swears you do more usurp
Than doth your brother that hath banished you.
Today my lord of Amiens and myself
Did steal behind him as he lay along
Under an oak, whose antique root peeps out
Upon the brook that brawls along this wood,

The First Lord describes how Jaques, watching a wounded deer, draws moral lessons about society from the stricken animal's plight. The duke looks forward to debating with Jaques.

1 Learning from nature (in pairs)

Duke Senior ended his first speech claiming that nature could teach all kinds of moral lessons about human life. Now he asks what lessons Jaques had drawn from the sight of a wounded stag ('Did he not moralise this spectacle?'). The First Lord lists three of Jaques' conclusions that criticise society:

Lines 46–9: The deer, weeping into a 'needless stream' (not needing: already full of water), is like someone who makes a will leaving money to a person who already has plenty.

Lines 49–52: The wounded deer, abandoned by the herd, is like a person struck by misfortune who is rejected by society ('part/The flux of company' = divide the stream of friends).

Lines 52–7: The sight of a well-fed herd ignoring the wounded deer is like well-off people who ignore a friend who has fallen on hard times.

Jaques then criticised the duke and his lords (lines 60–3). He condemned them as usurpers and tyrants who have robbed the deer of their god-given and natural rights ('assigned and native') to the forest, by hunting and killing them. Look back at what the duke said about deer hunting in lines 21–5. Suggest how he now reacts to hearing himself so strongly criticised.

2 What is Jaques like?

'The melancholy Jaques' will appear in Scene 5. Write a sentence describing your first impression of him from how he is reported opposite. Check your view as you gain more knowledge of Jaques.

---

sequestered separated
ta'en a hurt been wounded
leathern coat hide
Much markèd of carefully watched by
Augmenting adding to
testament will
velvet friend fallow deer
careless carefree
most invectively vehemently, critically
usurpers illegal rulers
cope meet, talk with

To the which place a poor sequestered stag
That from the hunter's aim had ta'en a hurt,
Did come to languish; and indeed, my lord,
The wretched animal heaved forth such groans
That their discharge did stretch his leathern coat
Almost to bursting, and the big round tears
Coursed one another down his innocent nose
In piteous chase; and thus the hairy fool,
Much markèd of the melancholy Jaques,
Stood on th'extremest verge of the swift brook,
Augmenting it with tears.

DUKE SENIOR But what said Jaques?
Did he not moralise this spectacle?

FIRST LORD O yes, into a thousand similes.
First, for his weeping in the needless stream:
'Poor deer', quoth he, 'thou mak'st a testament
As worldlings do, giving thy sum of more
To that which hath too much.' Then, being there alone,
Left and abandoned of his velvet friend:
''Tis right', quoth he, 'thus misery doth part
The flux of company.' Anon a careless herd,
Full of the pasture, jumps along by him
And never stays to greet him: 'Ay', quoth Jaques,
'Sweep on you fat and greasy citizens,
'Tis just the fashion. Wherefore do you look
Upon that poor and broken bankrupt there?'
Thus most invectively he pierceth through
The body of the country, city, court,
Yea, and of this our life, swearing that we
Are mere usurpers, tyrants, and what's worse,
To fright the animals and to kill them up
In their assigned and native dwelling-place.

DUKE SENIOR And did you leave him in this contemplation?

SECOND LORD We did, my lord, weeping and commenting
Upon the sobbing deer.

DUKE SENIOR Show me the place;
I love to cope him in these sullen fits,
For then he's full of matter.

FIRST LORD I'll bring you to him straight.

Exeunt

Duke Frederick thinks some of his servants have assisted Rosalind and Celia to flee. Touchstone is reported missing. Frederick orders Orlando or Oliver be brought to him, and the fugitives to be hunted down.

1 Contrasts

Shakespeare ensures that each scene contrasts with and comments on the scene that precedes it. Imagine you are directing the play. Work out how to show Scene 2 dramatically contrasting with or commenting on Scene 1 for each of the following:

- setting (the court versus the Forest of Arden);
- character (Duke Frederick versus Duke Senior);
- theme (both scenes have hunting as a theme).

2 Stage the scene (in small groups)

Scene 2 is very short, but it is vital to the play. It provides contrasts (see activity 1 above), insight into character and information to advance the plot. Rehearse and stage the scene as dramatically as you can. Think about: Are the lords afraid of Duke Frederick? What does he do as they speak? How does he deliver his instructions in the final five lines: for example, might his command 'Fetch that gallant hither' be dictated to a fearful scribe?

3 Hisperia's story

Hisperia, Celia's lady-in-waiting, never appears in the play and is not mentioned again. But she will have a point of view on what has happened. Step into role as Hisperia and tell all you know about events at the court up to this moment.

---

villeins minor servants
Are of consent and sufferance in this agreed and helped the plot
untreasured bereft (of Celia)
roinish coarse, scurvy
wont accustomed
parts and graces physical appearance and good manners
foil defeat
gallant young gentleman (Orlando)
inquisition enquiry
quail slacken, cease, fail

Act 2 Scene 2
Duke Frederick's palace

Enter DUKE FREDERICK with Lords

DUKE FREDERICK Can it be possible that no man saw them?
It cannot be: some villeins of my court
Are of consent and sufferance in this.

FIRST LORD I cannot hear of any that did see her;
The ladies, her attendants of her chamber,
Saw her abed and, in the morning early,
They found the bed untreasured of their mistress.

SECOND LORD My lord, the roinish clown, at whom so oft
Your grace was wont to laugh, is also missing.
Hisperia, the princess' gentlewoman,
Confesses that she secretly o'erheard
Your daughter and her cousin much commend
The parts and graces of the wrestler
That did but lately foil the sinewy Charles;
And she believes, wherever they are gone,
That youth is surely in their company.

DUKE FREDERICK Send to his brother: 'Fetch that gallant hither.'
If he be absent, bring his brother to me –
I'll make him find him. Do this suddenly,
And let not search and inquisition quail
To bring again these foolish runaways.

Exeunt

Adam bemoans the fact that Orlando's good qualities have made him hated in the unnatural world of the court. He reveals that Oliver plots to kill Orlando, and urges Orlando to leave.

1 First read through (in pairs)

In Scene 2, Duke Frederick was told that Orlando was sure to be with Celia and Rosalind. But Scene 3 shows that Orlando has returned home after the wrestling match (as he said he would at the end of Act 1, Scene 2). Adam greets him with threatening news. To gain a first impression, take parts and read the whole scene.

2 Old Adam

There is a story that Shakespeare himself played Adam at the Globe Theatre. If the story is true, how did he play the faithful old servant? Shakespeare was in his thirties, Adam is almost eighty years old.

Experiment with different ways of speaking Adam's first two speeches. The repetitions and questions in the language can help you create a stereotype of an old man, fearful and rambling, his mind sometimes wandering. Is that a portrayal you favour?

3 An unnatural world (in small groups)

Lines 2–6 portray Orlando's virtues ('gentle', 'sweet', and so on), but Adam goes on to tell how such good qualities are hated in the unnatural world of the court. Duke Frederick and Orlando's own brother envy and hate him for his virtues (just as Frederick hates Rosalind for her virtues).

Talk together about whether you think lines 10–15 are true today. Are some people disliked because they possess decency and goodness? Try to give actual examples of people whose virtues ('graces') create hostility in others.

memory reminder
fond foolish
bonny prizer champion prize-fighter
humorous duke moody Duke Frederick
graces virtues
sanctified blessed
comely beautiful, virtuous
Envenoms poisons
cut you off kill you
practices plots, deceits
Abhor hate

ACT 2 SCENE 3
Outside Oliver's house

Enter ORLANDO

ORLANDO Who's there?

[*Enter* ADAM]

ADAM What, my young master! O my gentle master,
O my sweet master, O you memory
Of old Sir Roland, why, what make you here?
Why are you virtuous? Why do people love you?
And wherefore are you gentle, strong, and valiant?
Why would you be so fond to overcome
The bonny prizer of the humorous duke?
Your praise is come too swiftly home before you.
Know you not, master, to some kind of men
Their graces serve them but as enemies?
No more do yours: your virtues, gentle master,
Are sanctified and holy traitors to you.
O what a world is this when what is comely
Envenoms him that bears it!

ORLANDO Why, what's the matter?

ADAM O unhappy youth,
Come not within these doors; within this roof
The enemy of all your graces lives
Your brother – no, no brother – yet the son –
Yet not the son, I will not call him son
Of him I was about to call his father –
Hath heard your praises, and this night he means
To burn the lodging where you use to lie
And you within it. If he fail of that,
He will have other means to cut you off:
I overheard him and his practices.
This is no place, this house is but a butchery:
Abhor it, fear it, do not enter it.

ORLANDO Why whither, Adam, wouldst thou have me go?

ADAM No matter whither, so you come not here.

Orlando prefers to face his murderous brother rather than become a beggar or highwayman. Adam offers his life savings and service to Orlando, who accepts and praises Adam's faithfulness.

---

1 Nobility or snobbery?

Orlando's determination to stay and face the murderous fury of his brother, rather than to beg or become a highwayman ('A thievish living on the common road') is usually interpreted as showing his bravery and nobility of character. Give your response to the student who wrote: 'lines 31–7 show Orlando as a bit of a snob'.

2 How to play Adam? (in pairs)

Adam offers his life savings to Orlando, saying that God will look after him. His words about God feeding the ravens and sparrows echo lines from the Bible (Matthew 10.29, Psalms 147.9). Some actors play Adam's lines for laughs. Tell each other what you think of each of these examples of stage business:

Line 45: 'Here is the gold' – producing a huge bucket of coins.

Line 47: 'I am strong and lusty' – almost fainting as he speaks.

Lines 48–51: gestures of refusing alcohol and sexual activity.

Line 53: 'Frosty but kindly' – tapping his white-haired head.

Lines 54–5: tottering as he speaks.

3 It was better in the olden times!

Lines 56–8 describe two characteristics of 'the antique world' (past times): 'service' was 'constant' (faithful), and 'for duty not for meed' (reward). Explain how this contrasts with Orlando's view of the modern world ('these times') in lines 59–63 ('the fashion … the having').

---

base and boisterous lowly and violent
a diverted blood an unnatural
thrifty hire wages
unregarded age disvalued old age
with unbashful forehead shamelessly
debility feebleness
a rotten tree (Orlando's image of himself)
In lieu of in return for
husbandry careful management
settled low content humble and contented way of living

ORLANDO What, wouldst thou have me go and beg my food,
Or with a base and boisterous sword enforce
A thievish living on the common road?
This I must do or know not what to do;
Yet this I will not do, do how I can.
I rather will subject me to the malice
Of a diverted blood and bloody brother.

ADAM But do not so: I have five hundred crowns,
The thrifty hire I saved under your father,
Which I did store to be my foster-nurse
When service should in my old limbs lie lame
And unregarded age in corners thrown;
Take that, and He that doth the ravens feed,
Yea providently caters for the sparrow,
Be comfort to my age. Here is the gold:
All this I give you; let me be your servant –
Though I look old, yet I am strong and lusty;
For in my youth I never did apply
Hot and rebellious liquors in my blood,
Nor did not with unbashful forehead woo
The means of weakness and debility;
Therefore my age is as a lusty winter,
Frosty but kindly. Let me go with you:
I'll do the service of a younger man
In all your business and necessities.

ORLANDO O good old man, how well in thee appears
The constant service of the antique world,
When service sweat for duty not for meed.
Thou art not for the fashion of these times
Where none will sweat but for promotion
And, having that, do choke their service up
Even with the having. It is not so with thee;
But, poor old man, thou prun'st a rotten tree
That cannot so much as a blossom yield,
In lieu of all thy pains and husbandry.
But come thy ways: we'll go along together
And, ere we have thy youthful wages spent,
We'll light upon some settled low content.

Adam resolves to be Orlando's faithful servant, and bids goodbye to his old home where he has lived for over sixty years. In Scene 4, Rosalind, Celia and Touchstone seem exhausted as they arrive in Arden.

1 Arrival in Arden (in pairs)

Lines 1–13 suggest that all three travellers are very weary and that Touchstone is disillusioned ('the more fool I!'). Experiment with speaking Rosalind's line 12 in different ways: 'Well, this is the Forest of Arden'. For example, what is the effect if she speaks 'this' incredulously?

'I cannot go no further'. Celia (centre) is exhausted, and Rosalind and Touchstone are dismayed at their first sight of the Forest of Arden.

fourscore eighty
Jupiter in Roman mythology, king of the gods (Ganymede was his page, see page 30)
weaker vessel woman (Celia)
doublet and hose jacket and breeches of the Elizabethan period
bear with/bear consider/carry
cross punishment, symbol on a coin (another of Touchstone's puns)
I have loved ere now I've been in love in the past

ADAM Master, go on, and I will follow thee
To the last gasp with truth and loyalty.
From seventeen years till now almost fourscore
Here lived I, but now live here no more.
At seventeen years many their fortunes seek,
But at fourscore it is too late a week;
Yet fortune cannot recompense me better
Than to die well and not my master's debtor.

Exeunt

Act 2 Scene 4
The Forest of Arden

Enter ROSALIND disguised as the boy GANYMEDE, CELIA disguised as a shepherdess ALIENA, and the clown TOUCHSTONE dressed in motley

ROSALIND O Jupiter, how merry are my spirits!

TOUCHSTONE I care not for my spirits, if my legs were not weary.

ROSALIND [*Aside*] I could find in my heart to disgrace my man's apparel and to cry like a woman; but I must comfort the weaker vessel, as doublet and hose ought to show itself courageous to petticoat; therefore – courage, good Aliena!

CELIA I pray you bear with me, I cannot go no further.

TOUCHSTONE For my part, I had rather bear with you than bear you; yet I should bear no cross if I did bear you, for I think you have no money in your purse.

ROSALIND Well, this is the Forest of Arden.

TOUCHSTONE Aye, now am I in Arden, the more fool I! When I was at home I was in a better place; but travellers must be content.

Enter CORIN *and* SILVIUS

ROSALIND Aye, be so, good Touchstone. Look you, who comes here:
A young man and an old in solemn talk.

CORIN That is the way to make her scorn you still.

SILVIUS O Corin, that thou knew'st how I do love her.

CORIN I partly guess, for I have loved ere now.

Silvius claims that no man's love can equal his, and that the behaviour of lovers is always extreme. Rosalind agrees with his words, but Touchstone's memories show the absurdities of lovers' behaviour.

---

1 Stereotypes or believably human?

Should Silvius and Corin be played as stereotypes, or realistically, as rounded human beings? Both are stock figures from the pastoral romance tradition that influenced Shakespeare as he wrote *As You Like It.* Silvius is the young shepherd suffering the pangs of unrequited love. His lines 27–37, with their repetitive, regularly patterned verse, seem suited to the stereotype. Corin is the wise and contented old father figure. Keep the question of how to play them in mind as you read on.

2 The foolishness of love

Silvius' expression of love reminds Rosalind of her own passionate feelings for Orlando. But Touchstone lampoons Silvius' words. He tells how his love for a milkmaid, Jane Smile, made him behave foolishly. He jealously attacked a stone that he thought to be his rival in love; kissed a wooden paddle ('batler') that Jane used to beat the clothes she washed; kissed the cow's udders ('dugs') that Jane's rough ('chapped') hands had milked; and presented her with pea pods ('peasecod') to wear as jewellery.

Touchstone's conclusion is that lovers do peculiar things ('run into strange capers'), and that just as everyone must die ('as all is mortal in Nature'), so it is inevitable that all lovers ('all nature in love') must behave foolishly ('mortal in folly').

Write a speech describing the foolish behaviour of a modern lover. Use the same style as Touchstone's parody.

---

fantasy love, desire
slightest folly smallest foolishness
Wearing thy hearer wearying your listener
broke from company run away from friends
searching of probing
hard adventure painful chance
ware aware
yond man yonder man (Corin)
kinsman relative, fellow clown

SILVIUS No, Corin, being old, thou canst not guess,
Though in thy youth thou wast as true a lover
As ever sighed upon a midnight pillow.
But if thy love were ever like to mine –
As sure I think did never man love so –
How many actions most ridiculous
Hast thou been drawn to by thy fantasy?

CORIN Into a thousand that I have forgotten.

SILVIUS O thou didst then never love so heartily.
If thou remembrest not the slightest folly
That ever love did make thee run into,
Thou hast not loved.
Or if thou hast not sat as I do now,
Wearing thy hearer in thy mistress' praise,
Thou hast not loved.
Or if thou hast not broke from company
Abruptly as my passion now makes me,
Thou hast not loved.
O Phebe, Phebe, Phebe! *Exit*

ROSALIND Alas, poor shepherd, searching of thy wound,
I have by hard adventure found mine own.

TOUCHSTONE And I mine: I remember when I was in love, I broke my sword upon a stone and bid him take that for coming a-night to Jane Smile; and I remember the kissing of her batler and the cow's dugs that her pretty chapped hands had milked; and I remember the wooing of a peasecod instead of her, from whom I took two cods and, giving her them again, said with weeping tears, 'Wear these for my sake.' We that are true lovers run into strange capers; but as all is mortal in Nature, so is all nature in love mortal in folly.

ROSALIND Thou speak'st wiser than thou art ware of.

TOUCHSTONE Nay, I shall ne'er be ware of my own wit till I break my shins against it.

ROSALIND Jove, Jove, this shepherd's passion
Is much upon my fashion.

TOUCHSTONE And mine, but it grows something stale with me.

CELIA I pray you, one of you question yond man
If he for gold will give us any food:
I faint almost to death.

TOUCHSTONE Holla, you, clown!

ROSALIND Peace, fool; he's not thy kinsman.

Rosalind asks where she may buy food and shelter. Corin tells that his miserly employer's property is for sale, and offers help. He agrees to buy the sheep farm with Rosalind's and Celia's money.

1 Superiority and embarrassment?

Is Rosalind embarrassed by Touchstone's air of superiority towards Corin ('Clown', 'Your betters')? Advise her how to speak 'Peace, I say'. Just how strong is her rebuke?

2 First test of disguise (in pairs)

This is the first time that Rosalind, disguised as a male, speaks to a stranger. Does Corin have suspicions about this young person he calls 'gentle sir'? Experiment with different ways of speaking Corin's line 63. Does he hesitate after his first three words, wondering just how to address this young boy, feminine in appearance?

3 Corin's point of view (in pairs)

Corin reveals that Arden has its unpleasant aspects. His employer is miserly ('of churlish disposition') and rarely thinks ('little recks') to do acts of kindness. In one production, to emphasise that at the cottage there was nothing suitable for Rosalind and Celia to eat, Corin fished in his pockets and pulled out the remains of an extremely stale loaf, which he broke in disgust as he emphasised 'you' in line 79.

Speak everything Corin says between lines 68–93. Show by expressions and gestures what Corin thinks of Celia's plight, of his master, of Silvius and of the prospect of working for Rosalind and Celia.

Good even good evening
prithee pray you
desert remote
entertainment food and shelter
succour help in distress
cot cottage
bounds of feed all his pastures
sheepcote cottage
in my voice for my part
swain lover
but erewhile just now
stand with honesty is fair dealing
mend increase
feeder shepherd, servant

CORIN Who calls?
TOUCHSTONE Your betters, sir.
CORIN Else are they very wretched.
ROSALIND [*To Touchstone*] Peace, I say –. Good even to you, friend.
CORIN And to you, gentle sir, and to you all.
ROSALIND I prithee, shepherd, if that love or gold
Can in this desert place buy entertainment,
Bring us where we may rest ourselves and feed.
Here's a young maid with travel much oppressed
And faints for succour.
CORIN Fair sir, I pity her
And wish, for her sake more than for mine own,
My fortunes were more able to relieve her;
But I am shepherd to another man,
And do not shear the fleeces that I graze.
My master is of churlish disposition
And little recks to find the way to heaven
By doing deeds of hospitality.
Besides, his cot, his flocks, and bounds of feed
Are now on sale, and at our sheepcote now
By reason of his absence there is nothing
That you will feed on. But what is, come see,
And in my voice most welcome shall you be.
ROSALIND What is he that shall buy his flock and pasture?
CORIN That young swain that you saw here but erewhile,
That little cares for buying anything.
ROSALIND I pray thee, if it stand with honesty,
Buy thou the cottage, pasture, and the flock,
And thou shalt have to pay for it of us.
CELIA And we will mend thy wages. I like this place
And willingly could waste my time in it.
CORIN Assuredly the thing is to be sold.
Go with me. If you like upon report
The soil, the profit, and this kind of life,
I will your very faithful feeder be,
And buy it with your gold right suddenly.

Exeunt

Amiens sings of the pleasure of forest life. Jaques asks for more singing, hoping it will add to his melancholy. He criticises the singing, politeness in general and Duke Senior.

---

1 Amiens' song (in small groups)

Amiens' song echoes the theme of Duke Senior's opening speech at the start of Act 2 ('Sweet are the uses of adversity'). No one knows the original music for 'Under the greenwood tree'. The first recorded melody was composed in 1740 by Thomas Arne for a production at the Drury Lane Theatre, London. Arne's setting has become traditional; you can find it and more about the songs in the play on page 180.

Make up your own music for the song, and devise a group delivery using repetitions, echoes and sound effects: rustling leaves, bird noises, rough weather noises, and so on.

2 Clues to Jaques' character? (in small groups)

Talk together about what each of the following suggests about Jaques' personality. How might his costume express his character?

Lines 11–12: he compares himself to a weasel, a small quarrelsome, sharp-toothed animal.

Line 14: he criticises Amiens' singing (and often gets a laugh from the audience).

Line 17: he seems interested only in the names of people who owe him money.

Lines 20–3: he compares politeness to baboons meeting each other, and detests gratitude because it sounds like a beggar's over-enthusiastic thanks.

Lines 27–9: he thinks Duke Senior too argumentative, and considers himself as intelligent as the duke, but more humble.

---

turn adapt, tune
note melody
Monsieur Sir (to signify Jaques high status, or to mock him?)
stanzo stanza, verse
'compliment' politeness
dog-apes baboons
cover the while lay the table meanwhile (prepare the picnic)
disputable argumentative

Act 2 Scene 5
The camp of Duke Senior

Enter AMIENS, JAQUES, and other Lords dressed as foresters

Song

AMIENS Under the greenwood tree,
Who loves to lie with me
And turn his merry note
Unto the sweet bird's throat:
Come hither, come hither, come hither:
Here shall he see
No enemy
But winter and rough weather.

JAQUES More, more, I prithee more.

AMIENS It will make you melancholy, Monsieur Jaques.

JAQUES I thank it. More, I prithee more. I can suck melancholy out of a song as a weasel sucks eggs. More, I prithee more.

AMIENS My voice is ragged: I know I cannot please you.

JAQUES I do not desire you to please me, I do desire you to sing. Come, more, another stanzo – call you 'em 'stanzos'?

AMIENS What you will, Monsieur Jaques.

JAQUES Nay, I care not for their names; they owe me nothing. Will you sing?

AMIENS More at your request than to please myself.

JAQUES Well then, if ever I thank any man, I'll thank you; but that they call 'compliment' is like th'encounter of two dog-apes. And when a man thanks me heartily, methinks I have given him a penny and he renders me the beggarly thanks. Come, sing; and you that will not, hold your tongues.

AMIENS Well, I'll end the song. – Sirs, cover the while; the duke will drink under this tree. – He hath been all this day to look you.

JAQUES And I have been all this day to avoid him: he is too disputable for my company: I think of as many matters as he, but I give heaven thanks and make no boast of them. Come, warble, come.

The exiled courtiers sing of the pleasures of leaving court and living simply in the country. Jaques' song mocks such pleasures, and implies that Duke Senior's followers are fools.

At the Globe Theatre on London's Bankside, Jaques listens glumly to Amiens' song.

1 To help your pronunciation

'Ducdame' is a nonsense word. Jaques makes it up like a 'Greek invocation' (a meaningless spell – 'It's all Greek to me') to gather the courtiers into a circle so that he can comment on their foolishness. All three songs in Scene 5 have the same structure and rhythm. So 'Ducdame' has the same three-syllable pattern as 'Come-hith-er' – 'Duc-dam-e'.

Who doth ambition shun whoever gives up court life
live i'th'sun live freely
in despite of my invention without using my imagination
A stubborn will to please to indulge his wilful fancies
rail against insult
the first-born of Egypt (in the Bible, God caused a plague, killing all Egypt's first-born children)
banquet light meal, picnic

Song. Altogether here

Who doth ambition shun
And loves to live i'th'sun;
Seeking the food he eats
And pleased with what he gets:

Come hither, come hither, come hither:
  Here shall he see
  No enemy
  But winter and rough weather.

JAQUES I'll give you a verse to this note that I made yesterday in despite of my invention.

AMIENS And I'll sing it.

JAQUES Thus it goes:

If it do come to pass
That any man turn ass,

Leaving his wealth and ease,
A stubborn will to please,

Ducdame, ducdame, ducdame.
  Here shall he see
  Gross fools as he,
And if he will come to me.

AMIENS What's that 'ducdame'?

JAQUES 'Tis a Greek invocation to call fools into a circle. I'll go sleep if I can: if I cannot, I'll rail against all the first-born of Egypt.

AMIENS And I'll go seek the duke: his banquet is prepared.

Exeunt

Wandering with Orlando in the forest, Adam fears he is near to death. Orlando comforts him and promises to find food and shelter. In Scene 7, Duke Senior is surprised at Jaques' cheerfulness.

---

1 How important is Scene 6? (in pairs)

Some critics argue that Scene 6 adds little or nothing to the play, and could be easily cut in performance. To discover if you agree or disagree with them, take parts as Adam and Orlando, speak the scene, then talk together about the following:

a Shakespeare ensures that every scene comments in some way (often ironically) on the preceding scene. How does Scene 6 relate to the ending of Scene 5?

b How might Scene 6 add to the audience's impression of the Forest of Arden?

c What does the scene reveal about Orlando's character?

d How could you stage Scene 6 to show its dramatic importance?

2 'Discord in the spheres'

When Duke Senior hears that the melancholy Jaques was 'merry, hearing of a song', he expresses wry surprise in lines 5–6. The duke thinks that Jaques' personality is full of discordant, jarring elements ('compact of jars'). If he is now merry, in harmony with himself ('grow musical'), the cosmos itself will be full of chaotic noise.

'Discord in the spheres' echoes the old belief that the earth was at the centre of the universe, surrounded by crystal spheres on which the sun, moon and planets orbited. As the spheres moved, they created harmonious music. If Jaques has become happy, it will create chaos in that heavenly order.

---

uncouth wild
conceit imagination
powers physical strength
presently very soon
desert remote place

Lords dressed like outlaws (see page 69)
discord in the spheres disharmony in the cosmos
look merrily? (the duke is amazed to see Jaques happy)

ACT 2 SCENE 6
The Forest of Arden

Enter ORLANDO and ADAM

ADAM Dear master, I can go no further. O, I die for food. Here lie I down and measure out my grave. Farewell, kind master.

ORLANDO Why, how now, Adam, no greater heart in thee? Live a little, comfort a little, cheer thyself a little. If this uncouth forest yield anything savage, I will either be food for it or bring it for food to thee. Thy conceit is nearer death than thy powers. For my sake be comfortable; hold death a while at the arm's end. I will here be with thee presently, and if I bring thee not something to eat, I will give thee leave to die; but if thou diest before I come, thou art a mocker of my labour. Well said, thou look'st cheerly, and I'll be with thee quickly. Yet thou liest in the bleak air. Come, I will bear thee to some shelter, and thou shalt not die for lack of a dinner if there live anything in this desert. Cheerly, good Adam.

Exeunt

ACT 2 SCENE 7
The camp of Duke Senior

Enter DUKE SENIOR, AMIENS, and Lords dressed like outlaws

DUKE SENIOR I think he be transformed into a beast,
For I can nowhere find him like a man.
AMIENS My lord, he is but even now gone hence;
Here was he merry, hearing of a song.
DUKE SENIOR If he, compact of jars, grow musical,
We shall have shortly discord in the spheres.
Go seek him; tell him I would speak with him.

Enter JAQUES

AMIENS He saves my labour by his own approach.
DUKE SENIOR Why, how now, monsieur, what a life is this
That your poor friends must woo your company?
What, you look merrily?

Jaques recounts how he enjoyed meeting Touchstone and listening to his moralising. He praises Touchstone, and wishes he were a fool, so that he can criticise whoever he wishes.

1 Meeting a fellow pessimist (in pairs)

Jaques' joy comes from meeting a cynic like himself who takes a negative view of the 'miserable world' (line 13) in which growing old and becoming corrupt are inevitable ('And so, from hour to hour, we ripe and ripe,/And then, from hour to hour, we rot and rot'). Jaques may also be amused at the sexual innuendo in Touchstone's words, for example, in Elizabethan times 'hour to hour' sounded the same as 'whore to whore'.

There are a number of contemporary echoes in Jaques' lines:

Line 19: recalls the Elizabethan proverb 'fortune favours fools'.

Line 28: 'and thereby hangs a tale' was a common saying and joke in Shakespeare's time (it also had a sexual meaning).

Line 39: because bread would quickly go stale on long voyages, ships used to carry hard biscuits for sailors to eat. At the end of a voyage, any left-overs (a 'remainder biscuit') would be very dry indeed.

Take turns to speak lines 12–43. Try to express Jaques' sardonic pleasure in meeting someone who confirms his jaundiced view of the world.

2 'Motley's the only wear'

Motley was the multicoloured patchwork costume of the professional fool or jester. You can find activities on Jaques' desire to wear motley (become a licensed fool) on page 58. There is a picture of a fool in motley on page 68.

---

railed on insulted, criticised
good set terms elegant and precise language
dial watch, sundial
poke pocket
Chanticleer a crowing rooster
sans intermission without break
observation proverbs
vents/In mangled forms speaks all jumbled up
suit request, garment
grows rank runs wild
Withal as well, also
gallèd offended, scarred

JAQUES A fool, a fool: I met a fool i'th'forest,
A motley fool – a miserable world –
As I do live by food, I met a fool
Who laid him down and basked him in the sun
And railed on Lady Fortune in good terms,
In good set terms, and yet a motley fool.
'Good morrow, fool', quoth I. 'No, sir', quoth he,
'Call me not fool till heaven hath sent me fortune.'
And then he drew a dial from his poke
And looking on it, with lack-lustre eye,
Says, very wisely, 'It is ten o'clock.
Thus we may see', quoth he, 'how the world wags:
'Tis but an hour ago since it was nine,
And after one hour more 'twill be eleven;
And so, from hour to hour, we ripe and ripe,
And then, from hour to hour, we rot and rot,
And thereby hangs a tale.' When I did hear
The motley fool thus moral on the time,
My lungs began to crow like Chanticleer
That fools should be so deep-contemplative;
And I did laugh, sans intermission,
An hour by his dial. O noble fool,
O worthy fool: motley's the only wear.

DUKE SENIOR What fool is this?

JAQUES A worthy fool: one that hath been a courtier
And says, 'If ladies be but young and fair,
They have the gift to know it'; and in his brain,
Which is as dry as the remainder biscuit
After a voyage, he hath strange places crammed
With observation, the which he vents
In mangled forms. O that I were a fool!
I am ambitious for a motley coat.

DUKE SENIOR Thou shalt have one.

JAQUES It is my only suit,
Provided that you weed your better judgements
Of all opinion that grows rank in them
That I am wise. I must have liberty
Withal, as large a charter as the wind,
To blow on whom I please: for so fools have.
And they that are most gallèd with my folly,
They most must laugh. And why, sir, must they so?

Jaques claims that people hurt by clever criticism should acknowledge the humour. He wants to cleanse the world with his satire, but the duke accuses him of hypocrisy. Jaques defends himself against the charge.

---

1 Would you laugh it off? (in small groups)

In lines 50–7, Jaques claims that the people he criticises would be wise to laugh and not ignore the criticism ('seem senseless of the bob'). Otherwise their foolishness will be exposed ('folly is anatomised') by even the most chance remarks ('squand'ring glances'). Talk together about whether you think it best to ignore clever but hurtful remarks, or to join in the laughter.

2 Jaques: satirist and hypocrite (in pairs)

Jaques wants to use his criticism like medicine, cleansing and curing the world's wrongs. The duke reveals Jaques' hypocrisy: he has been a philanderer ('libertine'), full of lust ('the brutish sting'). It would be a sin for Jaques, a sinner, to vomit ('disgorge') his own diseases upon others. Jaques defends himself, saying his satire is not directed at particular individuals, but at the vice itself, because a vice like pride is as widespread and universal as the sea. He gives two examples:

- If I criticise city women for wearing clothes too expensive and magnificent for them, no particular woman can complain, because all women ('her neighbour') do it.
- If a low-status man tells me to mind my own business when I criticise his fine clothes ('he of basest function … cost'), then either he demonstrates that my criticism is right, or the criticism applies to everyone ('my taxing like a wild goose … man').

Say why you think Shakespeare makes Jaques criticise clothes, rather than more serious examples of human folly.

---

very wisely hit cleverly criticise
smart is hurt
counter worthless coin
embossèd sores and headed evils scabs and boils
tax any private party criticise a particular individual
the weary very means do ebb it exhausts itself
cost of princes most expensive clothes
bravery fine clothes
suits … speech shows he is as foolish as I say he is

The why is plain as way to parish church:
He that a fool doth very wisely hit,
Doth very foolishly, although he smart,
If he seem senseless of the bob. If not,
The wise man's folly is anatomised
Even by the squand'ring glances of the fool.
Invest me in my motley; give me leave
To speak my mind, and I will through and through
Cleanse the foul body of th'infected world,
If they will patiently receive my medicine.

DUKE SENIOR Fie on thee! I can tell what thou wouldst do.

JAQUES What, for a counter, would I do but good?

DUKE SENIOR Most mischievous foul sin in chiding sin:
For thou thyself hast been a libertine,
As sensual as the brutish sting itself,
And all th'embossèd sores and headed evils
That thou with licence of free foot hast caught
Wouldst thou disgorge into the general world.

JAQUES Why, who cries out on pride
That can therein tax any private party?
Doth it not flow as hugely as the sea
Till that the weary very means do ebb?
What woman in the city do I name
When that I say the city-woman bears
The cost of princes on unworthy shoulders?
Who can come in and say that I mean her,
When such a one as she, such is her neighbour?
Or what is he of basest function
That says his bravery is not on my cost,
Thinking that I mean him, but therein suits
His folly to the mettle of my speech?
There then! How then? What then? Let me see wherein
My tongue hath wrongèd him. If it do him right,
Then he hath wronged himself; if he be free,
Why then my taxing like a wild goose flies
Unclaimed of any man. But who comes here?

Enter ORLANDO [*with sword drawn*]

ORLANDO Forbear, and eat no more!

JAQUES Why, I have eat none yet.

Orlando's threats are met with kindly words from the duke and scepticism by Jaques. Surprised by the duke's invitation to eat, Orlando explains his menacing behaviour, asks for pity and is granted hospitality.

---

1 Real menace? (in small groups)

Orlando bursts into the peaceful open air banquet with his sword drawn and speaking threatening words. Do you think his aggression should be staged seriously or with humour? Work on different versions of how Orlando might behave and speak (for example, full of genuine menace, or lacking confidence and obviously not meaning to carry out his threat). Find a style that you feel is appropriate to his character.

2 Showing disregard

In many productions, Jaques takes a bite of an apple as he speaks line 101. Some people claim that on Shakespeare's Globe stage he may have eaten a grape, because at that time 'reason' rhymed with 'raisin' (a raisin is a dried grape). What else might Jaques do to show his disdain for Orlando's threat?

3 Recalling better times (in pairs)

Orlando asks for pardon for his threatening appearance ('the countenance/Of stern commandment'). He makes a gentle plea for help, appealing to the duke to remember an earlier, better time. His appeal is made in formal, repetitive verse, and the duke replies in the same style.

Decide the mood you would wish to create in lines 105–26 (for example, nostalgic, kindly, and so on). Take parts and speak the lines in ways you think would evoke that mood.

---

necessity be served really hungry people are fed
You touched my vein at first your first point was accurate
inland bred brought up in the city
nurture good manners
countenance appearance
desert inaccessible remote place
knolled pealed, rung
goodman's neighbour's
engendered bred, caused
doe/fawn female deer/young deer (mother/child)

ORLANDO Nor shalt not, till necessity be served.
JAQUES Of what kind should this cock come of?
DUKE SENIOR Art thou thus boldened, man, by thy distress,
Or else a rude despiser of good manners
That in civility thou seem'st so empty?
ORLANDO You touched my vein at first: the thorny point
Of bare distress hath ta'en from me the show
Of smooth civility; yet am I inland bred
And know some nurture. But forbear, I say;
He dies that touches any of this fruit
Till I and my affairs are answerèd.
JAQUES And you will not be answerèd with reason, I must die.
DUKE SENIOR What would you have? Your gentleness shall force
More than your force move us to gentleness.
ORLANDO I almost die for food, and let me have it.
DUKE SENIOR Sit down and feed, and welcome to our table.
ORLANDO Speak you so gently? Pardon me, I pray you:
I thought that all things had been savage here
And therefore put I on the countenance
Of stern commandment. But whate'er you are
That in this desert inaccessible,
Under the shade of melancholy boughs,
Lose and neglect the creeping hours of time –
If ever you have looked on better days,
If ever been where bells have knolled to church,
If ever sat at any goodman's feast,
If ever from your eyelids wiped a tear,
And know what 'tis to pity and be pitied,
Let gentleness my strong enforcement be,
In the which hope, I blush, and hide my sword.
DUKE SENIOR True is it that we have seen better days,
And have with holy bell been knolled to church,
And sat at goodmen's feasts, and wiped our eyes
Of drops that sacred pity hath engendered:
And therefore sit you down in gentleness
And take upon command what help we have
That to your wanting may be ministered.
ORLANDO Then but forbear your food a little while
Whiles, like a doe, I go to find my fawn

Orlando leaves to fetch Adam.
The duke's comment that the world presents many sad scenes, inspires Jaques to describe the seven ages of man.

---

1 The seven ages of man (in groups of any size)

Prepare and act out your own version of lines 139–66 using some of the following suggestions.

a One person speaks the lines, the others mime each 'age'.

b Divide the speech into seven parts. Each small group takes responsibility for an 'age' and speaks and presents it.

c Construct a tableau (a frozen picture) to show the seven ages. The 'statues' stay perfectly still as one person speaks the lines.

d On stage, should Jaques speak to the duke and the courtiers, to the audience, or ...? Should he mime the ages as he speaks?

2 From cradle to grave – how realistic?

Jaques presents a very pessimistic vision of human life. Consider each age in turn and reply, with reasons, to the following questions.

- Do babies only cry and vomit? ('Mewling and puking')
- Do all schoolboys hate school?
- Are lovers foolish, writing sad songs or ridiculous poems?
- Are soldiers recklessly brave, seeking only brief fame ('the bubble "reputation"')?
- Do judges accept bribes? In Shakespeare's time a 'capon justice' was a judge who accepted a chicken ('capon') as a bribe.
- Do older men lack dignity, like the foolish old man of Italian comedy (Pantaloon)?
- Is the final picture of old age cynical and demeaning ('sans' = without)?

---

sufficed satisfied, fed
woeful pageants sad spectacles
pard leopard
Jealous in honour quick to take offence
wise saws moral sayings
modern instances trite examples
pouch purse
hose breeches
well saved carefully stored up
shrunk shank thin leg
treble high pitch
mere oblivion complete forgetfulness

And give it food: there is an old poor man
Who after me hath many a weary step
Limped in pure love. Till he be first sufficed,
Oppressed with two weak evils, age and hunger,
I will not touch a bit.

DUKE SENIOR Go find him out,
And we will nothing waste till you return.

ORLANDO I thank ye, and be blest for your good comfort. [*Exit*]

DUKE SENIOR Thou see'st we are not all alone unhappy:
This wide and universal theatre
Presents more woeful pageants than the scene
Wherein we play in.

JAQUES All the world's a stage
And all the men and women merely players:
They have their exits and their entrances
And one man in his time plays many parts,
His acts being seven ages. At first the infant,
Mewling and puking in the nurse's arms;
Then, the whining schoolboy with his satchel
And shining morning face, creeping like snail
Unwillingly to school; and then the lover,
Sighing like furnace, with a woeful ballad
Made to his mistress' eyebrow; then a soldier,
Full of strange oaths and bearded like the pard,
Jealous in honour, sudden, and quick in quarrel,
Seeking the bubble 'reputation'
Even in the cannon's mouth; and then the justice,
In fair round belly with good capon lined,
With eyes severe and beard of formal cut,
Full of wise saws and modern instances –
And so he plays his part; the sixth age shifts
Into the lean and slippered pantaloon,
With spectacles on nose and pouch on side,
His youthful hose well saved – a world too wide
For his shrunk shank – and his big manly voice,
Turning again toward childish treble, pipes
And whistles in his sound; last scene of all
That ends this strange eventful history
Is second childishness and mere oblivion,
Sans teeth, sans eyes, sans taste, sans everything.

Duke Senior invites Adam to eat. He calls for music. Amiens' song tells that nature, though harsh, is not so cruel as human ungratefulness; that most friendship is merely pretence, and most love, foolishness.

Adam and Orlando express their gratefulness to the duke, but Amiens sings of man's ingratitude.

venerable respected
fall to please start eating
rude rough
feigning pretending
holly symbol of joy and friendship at Christmas
nigh near, sharply
benefits forgot ingratitude, forgetting of good deeds
warp freeze

Enter ORLANDO *with* ADAM [*on his back*]

DUKE SENIOR Welcome. Set down your venerable burden,
And let him feed.

ORLANDO I thank you most for him.

ADAM So had you need: I scarce can speak
To thank you for myself.

DUKE SENIOR Welcome; fall to: I will not trouble you
As yet to question you about your fortunes. –
Give us some music, and, good cousin, sing.

Song

AMIENS Blow, blow, thou winter wind,
Thou art not so unkind
As man's ingratitude;
Thy tooth is not so keen,
Because thou art not seen,
Although thy breath be rude.
Hey-ho, sing hey-ho
Unto the green holly,
Most friendship is feigning,
Most loving mere folly.
The hey-ho, the holly,
This life is most jolly.

Freeze, freeze, thou bitter sky,
That dost not bite so nigh
As benefits forgot;
Though thou the waters warp,
Thy sting is not so sharp
As friend remembered not.
Hey-ho, sing hey-ho
Unto the green holly,
Most friendship is feigning,
Most loving mere folly.
The hey-ho, the holly,
This life is most jolly.

Duke Senior sees in Orlando's face the likeness of his old friend Sir Roland de Boys. He proposes that Orlando tells him the rest of his story later.

---

1 Dramatic ending (in pairs)

In the 1996 Royal Shakespeare Company production, Act 2 ended very dramatically. As the duke spoke his final line, all the characters moved towards Adam, only to find him dead. Everyone stared, frozen in dismay at the sight of Adam's body, and the lights faded to mark the interval in the performance. Talk together about what you think about that staging, then suggest how you would perform the final stage direction *Exeunt* (everyone leaves the stage).

2 Orlando tells his story

Duke Senior proposes to hear the rest of Orlando's story later. Step into role as Orlando and recount what has happened to you up to this moment in the play.

3 Dramatic contrasts

Shakespeare frequently dramatises contrasts (see pages 32, 69 and 70). Work out how you might stage the following potential contrasts:

- The sight of old Adam immediately after Jaques' description 'Sans teeth, sans eyes, sans taste, sans everything'. Does Adam's appearance confirm or deny Jaques' description?
- Amiens' song of human ingratitude, versus the gratitude Orlando and Adam express for the duke's hospitality.
- Amiens' song that friendship is feigning (pretence) versus the comradeship shown on stage (Orlando and Adam, the exiled court).

---

faithfully convincingly
effigies likeness, image
limned painted, portrayed
residue of your fortune rest of your story

DUKE SENIOR If that you were the good Sir Roland's son,
As you have whispered faithfully you were,
And as mine eye doth his effigies witness
Most truly limned and living in your face,
Be truly welcome hither. I am the duke
That loved your father. The residue of your fortune
Go to my cave and tell me. – Good old man,
Thou art right welcome as thy master is. –
[*To Orlando*] Support him by the arm. [*To Adam*] Give me your hand,
And let me all your fortunes understand.

Exeunt

Looking back at Act 2

Activities for groups or individuals

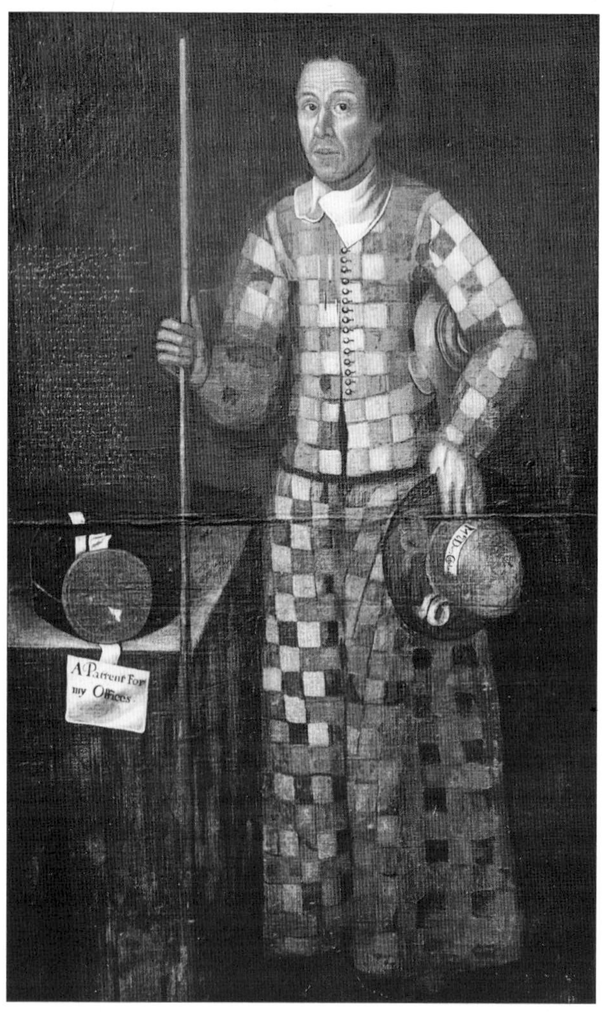

'Motley's the only wear'. In Scene 7, Jaques longs to play the role of clown and criticise the world. The illustration, painted about forty years after Shakespeare's death, shows Tom Skelton, a professional fool dressed in motley (a colourful patchwork costume). He worked for a rich family in Lancashire. Compare this picture with those of Touchstone on pages 33, 94, 109, 169 and 172.

1 Contrasts and juxtapositions

Act 2 continues Shakespeare's dramatic practice of inviting the audience to consider how the scene they are watching contrasts with and comments on the preceding scene. Check through the seven scenes of the Act suggesting how each is juxtaposed in some way with the one before. Keep in mind some of the contrasting themes of the play: court versus country, brother versus brother, virtue versus evil, friendship versus enmity. For example, Scene 1 is set in the forest and shows the banished duke contrasting forest life (good) with life at court (bad). The preceding scene was set in Duke Frederick's corrupt court, and it ended with Celia's cry 'not to banishment'.

2 Opportunities for design

The exiled lords appear dressed as 'foresters' or 'outlaws', and Amiens sings of 'the greenwood tree'. Sketch your designs for costumes for the 'outlaws' and the set for the forest. You will need to think about the season of the year. Is it winter, spring, or ...? Your decision will affect the mood you create through your designs (bleakness and cold, bittersweetness, and so on).

3 Learning from nature

At the start of Act 2, Duke Senior claims that nature can teach lessons in moral conduct to human beings. Two hundred years after Shakespeare wrote *As You Like It*, William Wordsworth expressed the same view in his poem 'The Tables Turned':

> One impulse from a vernal wood
> May teach you more of man,
> Of moral evil and of good,
> Than all the sages can.

Organise a class debate on the motion: 'Duke Senior and Wordsworth are right: there are "tongues in trees, books in the running brooks,/Sermons in stones, and good in everything".'

4 The seven ages of man

Remind yourself of Jaques' speech in Scene 7. Either write a parody of it as 'the seven ages of woman', or present two versions of the speech: the first showing human life as pleasant and kindly; the second showing it as undignified, harsh and foolish.

In Scene 1, Duke Frederick threatens Oliver and orders him to capture Orlando dead or alive. In Scene 2, Orlando hangs his love poems to Rosalind on trees, and praises her.

---

1 More contrasts

At the end of Act 2, Orlando and Duke Senior, two exiles banished by their brothers, were seen talking peacefully together. Now, in Act 3 Scene 1, their two wicked brothers appear, with Frederick behaving vindictively towards Oliver. The contrast of forest and court life is stark: there is companionship and harmony in Arden, but hatred and murderous intention at court. Make your own suggestion of how Scene 2 contrasts with Scene 1.

2 Two wicked brothers (in small groups)

Scene 1 is the final court scene in the play. From now on all the action takes place in the Forest of Arden. This is also the last time Duke Frederick appears. Productions therefore try to make Scene 1 as memorable as possible. In one staging, Oliver was thrown in by the lords, bleeding and battered. He had obviously been tortured. Work out how you would stage the scene to greatest dramatic effect.

3 Useful information? (in small groups)

Orlando appeals to the 'thrice-crownèd queen of night' to keep watch over ('survey') Rosalind, who rules his life. Talk together about how valuable it would be for the following note to be included in a theatre programme.

> 'In Roman and Greek mythology, the "thrice-crownèd queen" ruled three worlds (the heavens, the earth and the underworld) as Diana (or Artemis), goddess of chastity and hunting; Proserpina (or Persephone or Hecate), goddess of the underworld; and Luna (or Selene), goddess of the moon.'

---

absent argument missing subject (Orlando)
seizure taking, confiscating
quit acquit
brother's mouth (Orlando's testimony)
of such a nature whose job it is
Make an extent upon seize
expediently hastily
chaste virginal, pure
pale sphere moon
huntress' name (Rosalind)
sway rule
character write, carve
unexpressive she indescribable Rosalind

Act 3 Scene 1
Duke Frederick's palace

Enter DUKE FREDERICK, Lords, and OLIVER

DUKE FREDERICK 'Not see him since'? Sir, sir, that cannot be!
But were I not the better part made mercy,
I should not seek an absent argument
Of my revenge, thou present. But look to it:
Find out thy brother, wheresoe'er he is;
Seek him with candle; bring him dead or living
Within this twelvemonth, or turn thou no more
To seek a living in our territory.
Thy lands and all things that thou dost call thine
Worth seizure, do we seize into our hands
Till thou canst quit thee by thy brother's mouth
Of what we think against thee.

OLIVER O that your highness knew my heart in this:
I never loved my brother in my life.

DUKE FREDERICK More villain thou. Well, push him out of doors
And let my officers of such a nature
Make an extent upon his house and lands.
Do this expediently and turn him going. *Exeunt*

Act 3 Scene 2
The Forest of Arden

Enter ORLANDO with a sheet of paper in his hand

ORLANDO Hang there, my verse, in witness of my love;
And thou, thrice-crownèd queen of night, survey
With thy chaste eye, from thy pale sphere above,
Thy huntress' name that my full life doth sway.
O Rosalind, these trees shall be my books,
And in their barks my thoughts I'll character
That every eye which in this forest looks
Shall see thy virtue witnessed everywhere.
Run, run, Orlando, carve on every tree
The fair, the chaste, and unexpressive she. *Exit*

Touchstone, using clever-sounding language, tells that he likes and dislikes country life. Corin replies in the same empty manner. Touchstone claims Corin is damned for not having been at court.

---

1 Empty talk – court versus country

Scene 3 begins with a conversation on one of the major themes of the play: the comparison of country life with court life. To gain a first impression of how Shakespeare mocks the pretentious conversations that often took place among his own contemporaries, take parts as Touchstone and Corin and speak lines 1–64. Then use some of the activities below and on page 74 to help you work out how you would stage the dialogue.

a Touchstone's lines 2–9 are simply a series of statements saying that he both likes and dislikes country life ('good'/'naught', 'like'/'vile', and so on). Make up a few lines about your school or college using the same style.

b Does Touchstone treat Corin as an equal or as an inferior?

c Touchstone dresses up his empty language by calling it 'philosophy'. Corin answers him in the same high-sounding but superficial style, saying absurdly obvious things ('the property of rain is to wet', and so on). Is Corin mocking Touchstone, or is he serious about what he says?

d Touchstone makes a number of 'digs' (mocking jibes) at Corin. For example, 'a natural philosopher' could mean a foolish thinker, and 'an ill-roasted egg, all on one side' could be Touchstone's way of calling Corin half-baked. Decide whether Touchstone should share his sly humour with the audience.

e What stage business might accompany the conversation?

---

naught worthless
spare spartan, frugal
means employment
complain of good breeding protest he has had a poor upbringing
kindred family
Wast (line 17) were you
Nay, I hope I hope not
parlous perilous

ACT 3 SCENE 3
The Forest of Arden

Enter CORIN and TOUCHSTONE

CORIN And how like you this shepherd's life, Master Touchstone?

TOUCHSTONE Truly, shepherd, in respect of itself, it is a good life; but in respect that it is a shepherd's life, it is naught. In respect that it is solitary, I like it very well; but in respect that it is private, it is a very vile life. Now in respect it is in the fields, it pleaseth me well; but in respect it is not in the court, it is tedious. As it is a spare life, look you, it fits my humour well; but as there is no more plenty in it, it goes much against my stomach. Hast any philosophy in thee, shepherd?

CORIN No more but that I know the more one sickens, the worse at ease he is; and that he that wants money, means, and content is without three good friends; that the property of rain is to wet and fire to burn; that good pasture makes fat sheep; and that a great cause of the night is lack of the sun; that he that hath learned no wit by nature nor art may complain of good breeding, or comes of a very dull kindred.

TOUCHSTONE Such a one is a natural philosopher. – Wast ever in court, shepherd?

CORIN No, truly.

TOUCHSTONE Then thou art damned.

CORIN Nay, I hope.

TOUCHSTONE Truly thou art damned: like an ill-roasted egg, all on one side.

CORIN For not being at court? Your reason.

TOUCHSTONE Why, if thou never wast at court, thou never saw'st good manners; if thou never saw'st good manners, then thy manners must be wicked, and wickedness is sin, and sin is damnation. Thou art in a parlous state, shepherd.

Corin argues that to adopt court behaviour in the country would be foolish. Touchstone mocks the examples Corin gives. Corin expresses his contentment with country life, but Touchstone remains cynical.

---

1 Court and country matters

Corin denies that he is damned for not being at court. He claims it would be foolish to adopt court manners in the country. To kiss hands would be inappropriate, because shepherds' hands are greasy with handling the fleeces ('fells') of sheep, and are also stained with tar (used to heal wounds on sheep).

Touchstone rejects Corin's example, but his rejection is also a criticism of court manners. He points out that courtiers' hands are perfumed, and the perfume comes from civet, which is the secretion ('flux') from the anal gland of a wildcat.

a Is Touchstone contemptuous or humorous in his dismissals of Corin's examples as 'shallow'?

b Who comes off best in the exchange between Touchstone and Corin, or is it a draw?

2 Elizabethan jokes, modern audiences (in pairs)

Touchstone criticises breeding sheep as a sin, and calls Corin a pimp ('bawd') who brings together a young female sheep and a randy ('cuckoldly') old ram. Elizabethans loved jokes about cuckolds (deceived husbands) who were derided as having horns on their heads. Today, actors use all kinds of tricks to make a modern audience laugh. In one production, Touchstone stretched out 'ram' and 'match' in lines 60–1, bleating the 'a' sound like a sheep bleating: 'ra-a-a-a-m'. How would you deliver Touchstone's final speech?

Not a whit not a bit
salute greet
Instance give an example
worms' meat dead man
perpend consider
baser birth lowly origin
incision cut (to let knowledge enter)
raw unlearned
content with my harm accepting my hardships
bell-wether leading sheep of flock, with bell around neck
crooked-pated twisted horned

CORIN Not a whit, Touchstone: those that are good manners at the court are as ridiculous in the country as the behaviour of the country is most mockable at the court. You told me you salute not at the court but you kiss your hands: that courtesy would be uncleanly if courtiers were shepherds.

TOUCHSTONE Instance, briefly; come, instance.

CORIN Why, we are still handling our ewes, and their fells, you know, are greasy.

TOUCHSTONE Why, do not your courtiers' hands sweat, and is not the grease of a mutton as wholesome as the sweat of a man? Shallow, shallow! A better instance, I say – come.

CORIN Besides, our hands are hard.

TOUCHSTONE Your lips will feel them the sooner. Shallow again: a more sounder instance, come.

CORIN And they are often tarred over with the surgery of our sheep, and would you have us kiss tar? The courtiers' hands are perfumed with civet.

TOUCHSTONE Most shallow man! Thou worms' meat in respect of a good piece of flesh, indeed! Learn of the wise and perpend: civet is of a baser birth than tar, the very uncleanly flux of a cat. Mend the instance, shepherd.

CORIN You have too courtly a wit for me; I'll rest.

TOUCHSTONE Wilt thou rest damned? God help thee, shallow man. God make incision in thee, thou art raw.

CORIN Sir, I am a true labourer: I earn that I eat, get that I wear, owe no man hate, envy no man's happiness, glad of other men's good, content with my harm; and the greatest of my pride is to see my ewes graze and my lambs suck.

TOUCHSTONE That is another simple sin in you: to bring the ewes and the rams together and to offer to get your living by the copulation of cattle; to be bawd to a bell-wether and to betray a she-lamb of a twelvemonth to a crooked-pated old cuckoldly ram out of all reasonable match. If thou be'st not damned for this, the devil himself will have no shepherds. I cannot see else how thou shouldst 'scape.

CORIN Here comes young Monsieur Ganymede, my new mistress's brother.

Enter ROSALIND [*as* GANYMEDE]

Rosalind reads Orlando's poem in praise of her beauty. Touchstone composes a parody of the poem, full of sexual innuendo. Rosalind's reply puns jokingly at Touchstone's expense.

---

1 Touchstone's parody (in pairs)

Touchstone criticises Orlando's verses in praise of Rosalind as having the jogging, jerky rhythm of a procession of women riding to market ('the right butter-women's rack to market'). He makes up a burlesque in the same simple rhythm ('false gallop'). But where Orlando's love poem is idealised and spiritual, Touchstone's is all about the physical aspects of love.

To find how Touchstone follows the form of Orlando's poem, but alters the meaning, one person speak the first two lines that Rosalind reads, followed by the other person speaking the first two lines of Touchstone's parody. Repeat with the next two lines, and so on.

2 Actor's advice

Use this comment to help your delivery of Touchstone's poem:

> 'This is Shakespeare taking the mickey out of the tradition of courtly love. Touchstone's humour is of the "wink, wink, nudge, nudge" variety, full of sexual meaning. He probably pauses after every couplet to make sure that everyone gets the sexual implication of what he's saying, and to invent the next couplet.'

3 Does Rosalind know?

Rosalind's lines 95–6 pun on 'medlar' (a fruit best eaten when rotten) and 'meddler' (an interfering busybody). There is also a sexual joke, because medlar was Elizabethan slang for prostitute. Advise Rosalind how to speak the lines.

Western Inde West Indies
fairest lined (line 69) beautifully painted, drawn
eight years together for eight years without stopping
hart, hind stag, deer
after kind chase a female cat
lined (line 82) stuffed, padded out
sheaf and bind collect up and tie
to cart (the harvest and prostitutes were transported by cart)
graft implant

ROSALIND [*reading from a paper*]
'From the East to Western Inde
No jewel is like Rosalind;
Her worth, being mounted on the wind,
Through all the world bears Rosalind;
All the pictures fairest lined
Are but black to Rosalind;
Let no face be kept in mind
But the fair of Rosalind.'

TOUCHSTONE I'll rhyme you so eight years together, dinners and suppers and sleeping-hours excepted. It is the right butter-women's rack to market.

ROSALIND Out, fool!

TOUCHSTONE For a taste:
If a hart do lack a hind,
Let him seek out Rosalind;
If the cat will after kind,
So be sure will Rosalind;
Wintered garments must be lined,
So must slender Rosalind;
They that reap must sheaf and bind,
Then to cart with Rosalind;
Sweetest nut hath sourest rind,
Such a nut is Rosalind;
He that sweetest rose will find,
Must find love's prick – and Rosalind.
This is the very false gallop of verses: why do you infect yourself with them?

ROSALIND Peace, you dull fool. I found them on a tree.

TOUCHSTONE Truly, the tree yields bad fruit.

ROSALIND I'll graft it with you, and then I shall graft it with a medlar; then it will be the earliest fruit i'th'country, for you'll be rotten ere you be half ripe, and that's the right virtue of the medlar.

TOUCHSTONE You have said – but whether wisely or no, let the forest judge.

Enter CELIA [*as* ALIENA] *with a writing*

ROSALIND Peace, here comes my sister, reading. Stand aside.

Celia reads Orlando's poem which tells of the briefness of human life and of broken promises, but is mainly about how Rosalind embodies all beauty and grace. Rosalind calls it a boring sermon.

---

1 'Civil sayings' – echoes of Act 2

Orlando's poem says he will people the forest with proclamations ('Tongues') on every tree, containing wise maxims about society. Some will tell how human life is as short as the distance enclosed by a handspan. Others will tell of broken promises ('violated vows') between friends. Both echo earlier moments in the play. Turn back and read Touchstone's version (as reported by Jaques) of the first (Act 2 Scene 7, lines 20–8) and Amiens' song about the second (Act 2 Scene 7, lines 174–97).

2 Heavenly Rosalind (in pairs)

Orlando's praise of Rosalind compares her with famous women in Greek and Roman mythology or history:

Helen of Troy's beauty ('cheek') but not her unfaithfulness ('heart').

Cleopatra's majesty as Queen of Egypt.

Atalanta's speed (her 'better part'): in Greek mythology, this beautiful huntress was given the gift of speed. She vowed that any suitor who could not outrun her would be executed.

Lucretia's faithfulness: in Roman mythology, she killed herself to prove her honesty and devotion to her husband.

Work together as a modern Touchstone and replace lines 120–3 with four examples from today's world.

3 Stage business

In one production, Touchstone looked significantly at Rosalind and Celia as he spoke 'bag and baggage'. He snatched Orlando's poems from them at 'scrip and scrippage'.

---

erring pilgrimage wandering journey
Buckles in his sum of age encloses man's length of life
quintessence purest essence
sprite soul, spirit
in little in microcosm (in Rosalind)
Heaven Nature charged Heaven gave orders to nature
heavenly synod God's parliament
touches qualities
tedious homily boring sermon
Backfriends overhearers
scrip shepherd's purse

CELIA 'Why should this a desert be?
For it is unpeopled? No:
Tongues I'll hang on every tree,
That shall civil sayings show:
Some how brief the life of man
Runs his erring pilgrimage
That the stretching of a span
Buckles in his sum of age;
Some of violated vows
'Twixt the souls of friend and friend;
But upon the fairest boughs
Or at every sentence end
Will I "Rosalinda" write,
Teaching all that read to know
The quintessence of every sprite
Heaven would in little show.
Therefore Heaven Nature charged
That one body should be filled
With all graces wide-enlarged;
Nature presently distilled
Helen's cheek but not her heart,
Cleopatra's majesty,
Atalanta's better part,
Sad Lucretia's modesty.
Thus Rosalind of many parts
By heavenly synod was devised,
Of many faces, eyes, and hearts,
To have the touches dearest prized.
Heaven would that she these gifts should have,
And I to live and die her slave.'

ROSALIND [*Coming forward*] O most gentle Jupiter, what tedious homily of love have you wearied your parishioners withal, and never cried, 'Have patience, good people!'

CELIA How now? Backfriends! – Shepherd, go off a little. – Go with him, sirrah.

TOUCHSTONE Come, shepherd, let us make an honourable retreat, though not with bag and baggage, yet with scrip and scrippage.

Exeunt Touchstone and Corin

CELIA Didst thou hear these verses?

Rosalind and Celia joke about the lack of skill in the poems. Celia expresses amazement that Rosalind cannot guess who has written the verses. Rosalind begs to be told the poet's name.

1 But who is it? (in pairs)

The conversation between Rosalind and Celia is full of high spirits, teasing and excitement. Take parts and speak lines 137–212 straight through. Don't pause to worry about meaning (the conversation is full of ornate images that were typical of the romances of the time). After your reading, use the actors' advice below and the activities on page 82 to help you work out how to stage the episode.

a 'Rosalind's tone is pleading, breathless, self-tormenting. She's in love, and when you're in love you want to hear your lover talked about, so you stretch out the conversation. She knows very well that Orlando wrote the poems, but she pretends ignorance, to enjoy the pleasure of having Celia tease her about him.'

b 'Celia is incredulous: surely Rosalind must know who it is. She uses an exaggerated image that it is easier for mountains to meet than friends (lines 154–5), and she suggests in line 170 that Rosalind wants a sexual relationship with Orlando.'

c 'In lines 137–42, they joke about Orlando's bad poetry, with puns on "feet" (measures of metre in poetry) and "bear" (carry, or endure).'

d 'In lines 145–8, Rosalind says that her wondering was nearly over when Celia arrived (because she was at the seventh day of a "nine days' wonder" – a short-lived miracle). Her joke about Pythagoras and an Irish rat recalls the Greek philosopher who believed in the transmigration of souls (that a human being could live on as an animal), and the Elizabethan superstition that Irish magicians could kill rats by using rhyming spells.'

Trow you do you know
petitionary vehemence forceful begging
out of all hooping beyond all astonishment, delighted shouting
Good my complexion forgive my blushes
caparisoned dressed
disposition nature
South Sea of discovery incredibly long time
tidings news
stay wait for

ROSALIND O yes, I heard them all, and more too, for some of them had in them more feet than the verses would bear.

CELIA That's no matter: the feet might bear the verses.

ROSALIND Aye, but the feet were lame and could not bear themselves without the verse, and therefore stood lamely in the verse.

CELIA But didst thou hear without wondering how thy name should be hanged and carved upon these trees?

ROSALIND I was seven of the nine days out of the wonder before you came, for look here what I found on a palm-tree. I was never so berhymed since Pythagoras' time that I was an Irish rat – which I can hardly remember.

CELIA Trow you who hath done this?

ROSALIND Is it a man?

CELIA And a chain that you once wore about his neck? Change you colour?

ROSALIND I prithee, who?

CELIA O lord, lord, it is a hard matter for friends to meet, but mountains may be removed with earthquakes and so encounter.

ROSALIND Nay, but who is it?

CELIA Is it possible?

ROSALIND Nay, I prithee now, with most petitionary vehemence, tell me who it is.

CELIA O wonderful, wonderful, and most wonderful wonderful, and yet again wonderful, and after that out of all hooping.

ROSALIND Good my complexion, dost thou think, though I am caparisoned like a man, I have a doublet and hose in my disposition? One inch of delay more is a South Sea of discovery. I prithee tell me who is it – quickly, and speak apace. I would thou couldst stammer that thou mightst pour this concealed man out of thy mouth as wine comes out of a narrow-mouthed bottle: either too much at once or none at all. I prithee take the cork out of thy mouth that I may drink thy tidings.

CELIA So you may put a man in your belly.

ROSALIND Is he of God's making? What manner of man? Is his head worth a hat or his chin worth a beard?

CELIA Nay, he hath but a little beard.

ROSALIND Why, God will send more if the man will be thankful. Let me stay the growth of his beard, if thou delay me not the knowledge of his chin.

Celia reveals that Orlando wrote the poems. Rosalind's first thought is of her disguise as a man. She asks many eager questions and keeps interrupting Celia's story. They hide from Orlando and Jaques.

---

1 Quickfire questions (in pairs)

When Rosalind hears that Orlando is in the forest she wonders what she will do about her disguise as a man, then launches into a flurry of questions. Take turns to speak lines 184–8. How quickly can you deliver the lines with every word perfectly clearly spoken?

2 Head over heels? (in pairs)

Talk together about what 'head over heels in love' means to you. Does Rosalind's language show that the description applies to her?

3 A feminine trait?

Celia complains that Rosalind keeps interrupting her and should say 'Whoa!' ('holla') to her tongue which prances around ('curvets') like a frisky horse. She accuses Rosalind of adding a 'bourdon' (a refrain or accompaniment) to her story ('song'), and putting her off ('bring'st me out of tune'). Rosalind excuses herself by saying she is a woman: 'When I think, I must speak'.

Imagine the actor playing Rosalind says to you: 'I hate saying lines 209–10. It always gets a great laugh, but I think it's really sexist. It says women speak whatever is in their heads at the moment'. What do you reply?

4 Mood swings

How many different emotions has Rosalind expressed so far in this scene? Quickly review her speeches and suggest an emotion (or emotions) for each.

Wherein went he? what's he wearing?
What makes he here? what's he doing?
Gargantua giant (in a story by Rabelais, a 16th-century French author)
catechism set of religious questions and answers
atomies specks of dust
Jove's tree in Roman mythology, the oak, sacred to Jupiter
furnished dressed, equipped
heart (pun on 'hart', a deer)

CELIA It is young Orlando, that tripped up the wrestler's heels and your heart both in an instant.

ROSALIND Nay, but the devil take mocking! Speak sad brow and true maid.

CELIA I'faith, coz, 'tis he.

ROSALIND Orlando?

CELIA Orlando.

ROSALIND Alas the day, what shall I do with my doublet and hose? What did he when thou saw'st him? What said he? How looked he? Wherein went he? What makes he here? Did he ask for me? Where remains he? How parted he with thee? And when shalt thou see him again? Answer me in one word.

CELIA You must borrow me Gargantua's mouth first: 'tis a word too great for any mouth of this age's size. To say 'aye' and 'no' to these particulars is more than to answer in a catechism.

ROSALIND But doth he know that I am in this forest and in man's apparel? Looks he as freshly as he did the day he wrestled?

CELIA It is as easy to count atomies as to resolve the propositions of a lover; but take a taste of my finding him and relish it with good observance. I found him under a tree like a dropped acorn.

ROSALIND [*Aside*] It may well be called Jove's tree when it drops such fruit.

CELIA Give me audience, good madam.

ROSALIND Proceed.

CELIA There lay he stretched along like a wounded knight.

ROSALIND Though it be pity to see such a sight, it well becomes the ground.

CELIA Cry 'holla' to thy tongue, I prithee: it curvets unseasonably. He was furnished like a hunter.

ROSALIND O ominous: he comes to kill my heart.

CELIA I would sing my song without a bourdon; thou bring'st me out of tune.

ROSALIND Do you not know I am a woman? When I think, I must speak. Sweet, say on.

Enter ORLANDO *and* JAQUES

CELIA You bring me out. – Soft, comes he not here?

ROSALIND 'Tis he. Slink by, and note him.

[*Rosalind and Celia stand aside*]

Jaques and Orlando engage in a verbal fencing match, with Jaques criticising love. Orlando refuses to join Jaques in rebuking the world. They part, each mocking the other's folly: love and melancholy.

---

1 Polite insults (in pairs)

In the meeting between Jaques and Orlando, Shakespeare follows the conventions of courtly romance which often presented an encounter between two stock characters: the young lover and the older cynic. The two men end by mocking each other as those stereotypes: 'Signor Love', 'Monsieur Melancholy'.

Each man tries to score points off the other in politely phrased but insulting language. Take parts and speak the dialogue on the opposite page. Be as polite as you can, but have the intention of getting the better of your opponent.

2 Sentimental sayings

Lines 230–3 depend on knowledge that was familiar to Elizabethans, but is now virtually unknown. Jaques finds Orlando's answers trite and sentimental. He implies Orlando has made love to goldsmiths' wives and learned ('conned') his answers from the sentimental inscriptions that goldsmiths engraved inside rings. In reply, Orlando implies that Jaques spends his time in tavern bedrooms. These were hung with cheap imitation tapestries ('right painted cloth') with similar commonplace sayings painted on them. Where might you find collections of such sentimental sayings today?

3 Why does Jaques fall for it?

Orlando catches out Jaques in lines 242–6, by inviting him to look for a fool in the stream. Why does Jaques, the clever cynic, fall so easily into Orlando's trap?

---

as lief rather
God buy you goodbye (God be with you)
mar spoil
no mo no more
stature height
Atalanta very fast mover (see page 78)
rail against criticise, complain about
chide criticise
breather person
By my troth honestly
cipher nothing
tarry wait, stay

JAQUES I thank you for your company, but, good faith, I had as lief have been myself alone.

ORLANDO And so had I. But yet, for fashion sake, I thank you too for your society.

JAQUES God buy you. Let's meet as little as we can.

ORLANDO I do desire we may be better strangers.

JAQUES I pray you mar no more trees with writing love-songs in their barks.

ORLANDO I pray you mar no mo of my verses with reading them ill-favouredly.

JAQUES 'Rosalind' is your love's name?

ORLANDO Yes, just.

JAQUES I do not like her name.

ORLANDO There was no thought of pleasing you when she was christened.

JAQUES What stature is she of?

ORLANDO Just as high as my heart.

JAQUES You are full of pretty answers: have you not been acquainted with goldsmiths' wives and conned them out of rings?

ORLANDO Not so; but I answer you right painted cloth, from whence you have studied your questions.

JAQUES You have a nimble wit; I think 'twas made of Atalanta's heels. Will you sit down with me, and we two will rail against our mistress the world and all our misery.

ORLANDO I will chide no breather in the world but myself, against whom I know most faults.

JAQUES The worst fault you have is to be in love.

ORLANDO 'Tis a fault I will not change for your best virtue: I am weary of you.

JAQUES By my troth, I was seeking for a fool, when I found you.

ORLANDO He is drowned in the brook: look but in, and you shall see him.

JAQUES There I shall see mine own figure.

ORLANDO Which I take to be either a fool or a cipher.

JAQUES I'll tarry no longer with you. Farewell, good Signor Love.

ORLANDO I am glad of your departure. Adieu, good Monsieur Melancholy.

[*Exit Jaques*]

Rosalind, using her disguise as a young man, playfully tells Orlando how time moves at different speeds for different people. He expresses surprise at her refined accent.

1 First meeting (in pairs)

To gain an initial impression of Rosalind's meeting with Orlando, take parts and speak from line 250 to the end of the scene. Keep in mind the following comment by an actor:

> 'Rosalind now really tests her disguise. Will she be recognised by the man she loves? She has to speak and act like a man, but all the time she is teasing Orlando. The audience shares her pleasure and delight as she gets away with the deception. But at times she might come dangerously close to being found out! Rosalind conceals her true feelings for Orlando. She hides them behind witty language and play-acting. But the audience knows how she feels, as does Celia.'

2 Different speeds of time

Rosalind catches Orlando's interest by saying the sighing and groaning of a true lover would tell the time as well as a clock. She tells how time travels at different speeds for different people:

- the young woman for whom time 'trots hard' (lengthily and uncomfortably) between her engagement and her wedding day;
- the uneducated priest and the rich man for whom 'Time ambles' because both have an easy life: the priest is not tired by study, and the rich man is not oppressed by poverty;
- the criminal for whom 'Time gallops' as he awaits execution;
- the lawyers on holiday between court sessions ('term and term'), for whom time stands still.

Invent your own catalogue of people for whom time moves at different speeds.

saucy lackey cheeky servant
habit disguise
diverse various
withal with
sennight week (seven nights)
heavy tedious penury sad dull poverty
skirts outskirts, fringes
cony rabbit
kindled born
purchase acquire
removed remote (from court)

ROSALIND I will speak to him like a saucy lackey, and under that habit play the knave with him. [*To Orlando*] Do you hear, forester?

ORLANDO Very well. What would you?

ROSALIND I pray you, what is't o'clock?

ORLANDO You should ask me what time o'day: there's no clock in the forest.

ROSALIND Then there is no true lover in the forest, else sighing every minute and groaning every hour would detect the lazy foot of Time as well as a clock.

ORLANDO And why not the swift foot of Time? Had not that been as proper?

ROSALIND By no means, sir. Time travels in diverse paces with diverse persons. I'll tell you who Time ambles withal, who Time trots withal, who Time gallops withal, and who he stands still withal.

ORLANDO I prithee, who doth he trot withal?

ROSALIND Marry, he trots hard with a young maid between the contract of her marriage and the day it is solemnised. If the interim be but a sennight, Time's pace is so hard that it seems the length of seven year.

ORLANDO Who ambles Time withal?

ROSALIND With a priest that lacks Latin, and a rich man that hath not the gout; for the one sleeps easily because he cannot study, and the other lives merrily because he feels no pain; the one lacking the burden of lean and wasteful learning, the other knowing no burden of heavy tedious penury. These Time ambles withal.

ORLANDO Who doth he gallop withal?

ROSALIND With a thief to the gallows; for though he go as softly as foot can fall, he thinks himself too soon there.

ORLANDO Who stays it still withal?

ROSALIND With lawyers in the vacation; for they sleep between term and term, and then they perceive not how Time moves.

ORLANDO Where dwell you, pretty youth?

ROSALIND With this shepherdess, my sister, here in the skirts of the forest, like fringe upon a petticoat.

ORLANDO Are you native of this place?

ROSALIND As the cony that you see dwell where she is kindled.

ORLANDO Your accent is something finer than you could purchase in so removed a dwelling.

Rosalind says she was taught to speak by a well-educated uncle who also taught her the folly of love. She accuses Orlando of not looking like a man in love.

---

1 The signs of love

Rosalind lists eight signs by which a man in love can be recognised (a sunken cheek, dark circles around the eyes, and so on). All are the marks of someone who does not give a thought to their appearance ('careless desolation'). In *The Two Gentlemen of Verona*, Shakespeare gave another eight-item list of the marks of a lover:

> 'to wreathe your arms like a malcontent; to relish a love-song like a robin-redbreast; to walk alone like one that had the pestilence; to sigh like a schoolboy that had lost his ABC; to weep like a young wench that had buried her grandam; to fast like one that takes diet; to watch like one that fears robbing; to speak puling like a beggar at Hallowmas.'

Write out in your own words the eight items in lines 312–18. Compare them with the eight items from *The Two Gentlemen of Verona*. Then make up your own list of eight items by which someone in love can be recognised.

2 Sharing with the audience?

Does Rosalind share with the audience her delight in her disguise? At line 321, Orlando says that he wishes he could make Ganymede believe that he is in love. Rosalind's reply is full of ambiguities. Suggest what she might do to heighten the audience's enjoyment of her disguise as Ganymede as she speaks lines 322–4: 'Me believe it? You may as soon make her that you love believe it, which I warrant she is apter to do than to confess she does.'

---

inland city
courtship court life, wooing
taxed accused
physic medicine, advice
odes, elegies serious poems, love poems
fancy-monger trader in love
quotidian daily recurring fever
cage of rushes weak prison
unquestionable grumpy
your having ... revenue your beard is as small as a younger brother's income
point-device in your accoutrements neat and precise in your dress
still give ... consciences always lie about their feelings

ROSALIND I have been told so of many; but indeed an old religious uncle of mine taught me to speak, who was in his youth an inland man, one that knew courtship too well, for there he fell in love. I have heard him read many lectures against it, and I thank God I am not a woman to be touched with so many giddy offences as he hath generally taxed their whole sex withal.

ORLANDO Can you remember any of the principal evils that he laid to the charge of women?

ROSALIND There were none principal; they were all like one another as halfpence are, every one fault seeming monstrous till his fellow-fault came to match it.

ORLANDO I prithee recount some of them.

ROSALIND No. I will not cast away my physic but on those that are sick. There is a man haunts the forest that abuses our young plants with carving 'Rosalind' on their barks; hangs odes upon hawthorns and elegies on brambles; all, forsooth, defying the name of Rosalind. If I could meet that fancy-monger, I would give him some good counsel, for he seems to have the quotidian of love upon him.

ORLANDO I am he that is so love-shaked. I pray you tell me your remedy.

ROSALIND There is none of my uncle's marks upon you. He taught me how to know a man in love, in which cage of rushes I am sure you are not prisoner.

ORLANDO What were his marks?

ROSALIND A lean cheek, which you have not; a blue eye and sunken, which you have not; an unquestionable spirit, which you have not; a beard neglected, which you have not – but I pardon you for that, for, simply, your having in beard is a younger brother's revenue. Then your hose should be ungartered, your bonnet unbanded, your sleeve unbuttoned, your shoe untied, and everything about you demonstrating a careless desolation. But you are no such man; you are rather point-device in your accoutrements, as loving yourself than seeming the lover of any other.

ORLANDO Fair youth, I would I could make thee believe I love.

ROSALIND Me believe it? You may as soon make her that you love believe it, which I warrant she is apter to do than to confess she does. That is one of the points in the which women still give the lie to their consciences. But, in good sooth, are you he that hangs the verses on the trees wherein Rosalind is so admired?

Rosalind tells how, as Ganymede, she once cured a lover by pretending to be his love and behaving capriciously. This drove the lover insane, and he became a monk. Orlando agrees to follow her cure.

1 The cure for madness

In Elizabethan times, the mentally ill were thought to be possessed by devils. They were labelled as mad, locked in a dark room and whipped to drive out the devils. You can find how Shakespeare put this treatment on stage in *Twelfth Night* (Act 4 Scene 2) where Malvolio is called mad and locked in a dark room.

2 The cure for love (in groups of three)

Rosalind lists at least seventeen moods or actions that she used to 'cure' a lover. One person slowly speaks lines 336–46, pausing as each mood or action is named. The others, as Ganymede and the lover, mime what happened.

3 Three staging decisions (in groups of three)

a At line 349, Orlando refuses to undergo a cure for love, but in line 352, he agrees. Just how does Rosalind get him to change his mind by how she speaks and behaves at lines 350–1?

b In one production, Orlando gave Rosalind a hearty slap on the back at line 355, making her line 356 a kind of rebuke. How would you stage the final few lines?

c 'Come sister'. Celia has not spoken a word throughout Rosalind's conversation with Orlando. What has she been doing? Work out how she reacts as she watches Rosalind's play-acting, and how she finally leaves the stage.

---

moonish changeable like the moon
apish full of tricks
for every passion … anything showing all passions, but feeling none sincerely
cattle of this colour creatures like this
forswear him break my promises to him
drave drove
nook, merely monastic remote place, as a monk
liver (seat of the passions)
cot cottage

ORLANDO I swear to thee, youth, by the white hand of Rosalind, I am that he, that unfortunate he.

ROSALIND But are you so much in love as your rhymes speak?

ORLANDO Neither rhyme nor reason can express how much.

ROSALIND Love is merely a madness and, I tell you, deserves as well a dark-house and a whip as madmen do; and the reason why they are not so punished and cured is that the lunacy is so ordinary that the whippers are in love too. Yet I profess curing it by counsel.

ORLANDO Did you ever cure any so?

ROSALIND Yes, one, and in this manner. He was to imagine me his love, his mistress, and I set him every day to woo me. At which time would I, being but a moonish youth, grieve, be effeminate, changeable, longing and liking, proud, fantastical, apish, shallow, inconstant, full of tears, full of smiles; for every passion something, and for no passion truly anything, as boys and women are, for the most part, cattle of this colour; would now like him, now loathe him; then entertain him, then forswear him; now weep for him, then spit at him; that I drave my suitor from his mad humour of love to a living humour of madness, which was to forswear the full stream of the world and to live in a nook, merely monastic. And thus I cured him, and this way will I take upon me to wash your liver as clean as a sound sheep's heart, that there shall not be one spot of love in't.

ORLANDO I would not be cured, youth.

ROSALIND I would cure you if you would but call me Rosalind and come every day to my cot and woo me.

ORLANDO Now, by the faith of my love, I will. Tell me where it is.

ROSALIND Go with me to it and I'll show it you; and by the way you shall tell me where in the forest you live. Will you go?

ORLANDO With all my heart, good youth.

ROSALIND Nay, you must call me 'Rosalind'. – Come, sister, will you go?

Exeunt

Touchstone's literary jokes are lost on Audrey, although they amuse Jaques. Touchstone reflects that lovers and poets are both given to deception. He says he intends to marry Audrey.

---

1 Contrasts in love (in groups of three)

After the meeting of Rosalind and Orlando in Scene 3, Shakespeare now presents a lampoon of love. Audrey, the goatherd, is quite unlike Rosalind, and her wooing by Touchstone is very down-to-earth. Use the following suggestions, together with the activities on pages 94 and 96, to help you stage the scene.

a What is Audrey like? Many productions present her as simple-minded, dressed in old tattered clothes, her face begrimed with dirt, and speaking in a rustic accent. Is she really like that?

b In lines 5–6, 'goats' and 'Goths' had the same pronunciation in Shakespeare's time. Ovid was a Roman poet (43BC–17AD) who was sent into exile among the Goths, perhaps because of his erotic poetry and sexual misbehaviour (for Elizabethans, 'capricious' meant goat-like or lustful).

c Jaques understands Touchstone's classical reference, and mentions a story by Ovid in which Jupiter (Jove) was given hospitality in a thatched house. But Touchstone's joke passes Audrey by, and his lines 8–11 seem prompted by her lack of understanding. He says that her lack of response is like paying a huge bill for poor accommodation ('it strikes a man … room'). This may also be a reference to the death of Shakespeare's contemporary, the playwright Christopher Marlowe, who was killed in 1593 in an inn room in an argument over a tavern bill (see page 104).

Come apace hurry up
simple feature appearance
warrant protect
seconded supported by
forward child clever offspring
poetical knowing about literature (or about sex)
honest not sexually experienced, truthful
feigning deceitful, imaginative
hard-favoured ugly
material practical
couple marry
fain gladly

Act 3 Scene 4
The Forest of Arden

Enter TOUCHSTONE, AUDREY, with JAQUES behind, watching them

TOUCHSTONE Come apace, good Audrey; I will fetch up your goats, Audrey. And how, Audrey, am I the man yet? Doth my simple feature content you?

AUDREY Your features, Lord warrant us – what features?

TOUCHSTONE I am here with thee and thy goats as the most capricious poet honest Ovid was among the Goths.

JAQUES O knowledge ill-inhabited, worse than Jove in a thatched house!

TOUCHSTONE When a man's verses cannot be understood, nor a man's good wit seconded with the forward child, understanding, it strikes a man more dead than a great reckoning in a little room. Truly, I would the gods had made thee poetical.

AUDREY I do not know what 'poetical' is. Is it honest in deed and word? Is it a true thing?

TOUCHSTONE No, truly; for the truest poetry is the most feigning, and lovers are given to poetry; and what they swear in poetry may be said, as lovers, they do feign.

AUDREY Do you wish then that the gods had made me poetical?

TOUCHSTONE I do, truly; for thou swear'st to me thou art honest. Now if thou wert a poet, I might have some hope thou didst feign.

AUDREY Would you not have me honest?

TOUCHSTONE No, truly, unless thou wert hard-favoured: for honesty coupled to beauty is to have honey a sauce to sugar.

JAQUES A material fool.

AUDREY Well, I am not fair, and therefore I pray the gods make me honest.

TOUCHSTONE Truly, and to cast away honesty upon a foul slut were to put good meat into an unclean dish.

AUDREY I am not a slut, though I thank the gods I am foul.

TOUCHSTONE Well, praised be the gods for thy foulness: sluttishness may come hereafter. But be it as it may be, I will marry thee, and to that end I have been with Sir Oliver Martext, the vicar of the next village, who hath promised to meet me in this place of the forest and to couple us.

JAQUES I would fain see this meeting.

Touchstone implies that all women are unfaithful, but says it is better to be a married man than a bachelor. Jaques warns against Sir Oliver, but Touchstone sees advantages in a bad priest.

Audrey and Touchstone. Elizabethans loved jokes about horns: the sign of a deceived husband. Touchstone's lines 36–47 play with the idea ('horn-beasts' = forest stags, 'rascal' = weak or young deer). He says many husbands are cuckolded but do not know it, because all women are inevitably unfaithful ('that is the dowry of his wife' = that is what a wife brings to a marriage). Rich men and poor men alike are cuckolded. But even a cuckold is better than a bachelor, just as a fortified city is better than a village.

stagger stumble
dispatch marry
Monsieur What-Ye-Call't Jaques = jakes = Elizabethan word for lavatory
God'ild you God reward you
toy in hand trifle (Audrey? marriage?)
be covered put your hat on
bow, curb yoke, bit (restraints)
bells (which enable a falcon to be found and recaptured)
bill rub beaks
wainscot wood panelling

AUDREY Well, the gods give us joy.

TOUCHSTONE Amen. A man may, if he were of a fearful heart, stagger in this attempt; for here we have no temple but the wood, no assembly but horn-beasts. But what though? Courage! As horns are odious, they are necessary. It is said, 'Many a man knows no end of his goods.' Right: many a man has good horns and knows no end of them. Well, that is the dowry of his wife, 'tis none of his own getting. Horns? Even so. Poor men alone? No, no: the noblest deer hath them as huge as the rascal. Is the single man therefore blessed? No: as a walled town is more worthier than a village, so is the forehead of a married man more honourable than the bare brow of a bachelor. And, by how much defence is better than no skill, by so much is a horn more precious than to want.

Enter SIR OLIVER MARTEXT

Here comes Sir Oliver. – Sir Oliver Martext, you are well met. Will you dispatch us here under this tree, or shall we go with you to your chapel?

MARTEXT Is there none here to give the woman?

TOUCHSTONE I will not take her on gift of any man.

MARTEXT Truly, she must be given, or the marriage is not lawful.

JAQUES Proceed, proceed: I'll give her.

TOUCHSTONE Good-even, good Monsieur What-Ye-Call't. How do you, sir? You are very well met. God'ild you for your last company; I am very glad to see you. Even a toy in hand here, sir.

[*Jaques removes his hat*]

Nay, pray be covered.

JAQUES Will you be married, motley?

TOUCHSTONE As the ox hath his bow, sir, the horse his curb, and the falcon her bells, so man hath his desires, and as pigeons bill, so wedlock would be nibbling.

JAQUES And will you, being a man of your breeding, be married under a bush like a beggar? Get you to church, and have a good priest that can tell you what marriage is. This fellow will but join you together as they join wainscot, then one of you will prove a shrunk panel and, like green timber, warp, warp.

TOUCHSTONE I am not in the mind; but I were better to be married of him than of another, for he is not like to marry me well and, not being well married, it will be a good excuse for me hereafter to leave my wife.

Touchstone's song mocks Sir Oliver who claims he is not put off by such foolery. In Scene 5, Celia makes fun of Rosalind's distress over Orlando's non-appearance.

---

1 Mocking Sir Oliver (in groups of four)

Touchstone often accompanies his song (sometimes also sung by Audrey) with a dance around Sir Oliver. In one production, Oliver fell into a pool as a result of Touchstone's 'fantastical' tricks. Make up your own music for the song, and work out how you would stage the final twelve lines of Scene 4.

2 Rosalind drops her disguise (in pairs)

In earlier scenes, it was Rosalind who mocked the foolishness of love. Now it is Celia's turn. Because the two are alone, Rosalind drops her disguise as Ganymede and gives way to her feelings. She is close to tears, downcast because Orlando has not appeared. Celia mocks her moodiness by exaggeratedly agreeing with whatever Rosalind says, even comparing Orlando with Judas, the disciple who, in the Bible, betrayed Jesus with a kiss.

Take parts as Celia and Rosalind and speak lines 1–37 using the following comment to guide you:

> 'Rosalind is head over heels in love with Orlando and is fretful and emotional because he hasn't turned up. She's in an agony of frustration. All thoughts of her male disguise are forgotten as she gives way to her feelings. But Celia won't take her seriously, and ridicules everything she says. Rosalind lays herself open to Celia's friendly needling because she switches abruptly from criticising Orlando to defending him. Celia simply follows each mood swing with mocking replies.'

---

in bawdry immorally
Wind away wander off
fantastical knave crazy villain
flout me out of my calling trick me out of my job
become suit
dissembling deceiving
Judas (sometimes depicted with chestnut-coloured hair)
sanctity sacredness, purity
holy bread bread blessed in church
cast lips lips as cold as a statue's
Diana in Roman mythology, the goddess of chastity

JAQUES Go thou with me and let me counsel thee.

TOUCHSTONE Come, sweet Audrey, we must be married or we must live in bawdry. – Farewell, good Master Oliver. Not

[*Sings*] O sweet Oliver,
O brave Oliver,
Leave me not behind thee;

but [*Sings*]

Wind away,
Begone, I say,
I will not to wedding with thee.

MARTEXT [*Aside*] 'Tis no matter; ne'er a fantastical knave of them all shall flout me out of my calling.

Exeunt

ACT 3 SCENE 5
Outside the cottage of Rosalind and Celia

Enter ROSALIND (disguised as GANYMEDE) and CELIA (disguised as ALIENA)

ROSALIND Never talk to me; I will weep.

CELIA Do, I prithee; but yet have the grace to consider that tears do not become a man.

ROSALIND But have I not cause to weep?

CELIA As good cause as one would desire: therefore weep.

ROSALIND His very hair is of the dissembling colour.

CELIA Something browner than Judas's: marry, his kisses are Judas's own children.

ROSALIND I'faith, his hair is of a good colour.

CELIA An excellent colour: your chestnut was ever the only colour.

ROSALIND And his kissing is as full of sanctity as the touch of holy bread.

CELIA He hath bought a pair of cast lips of Diana. A nun of winter's sisterhood kisses not more religiously: the very ice of chastity is in them.

ROSALIND But why did he swear he would come this morning and comes not?

Celia doubts whether Orlando is truly in love. Rosalind recounts how she met her father, Duke Senior, who failed to recognise her. Corin invites them to watch Silvius attempting to woo Phebe.

1 Make them laugh

Celia's teasing of Rosalind contains many opportunities for humour. Work out how you could make the audience laugh at line 26 ('Was' is not 'is'), and at Celia's six uses of 'brave' and 'bravely' in lines 33–7 (they are highly ironic and mean something like 'fine' or 'wonderful').

2 What is a lover like?

Celia gives very unflattering descriptions of Orlando. He is:

- as hollow as an empty wineglass or nutshell (lines 21–2);
- like a cheating bartender who adds up the bill wrongly, and so gives a wrong description (lines 26–8);
- like a weak and cowardly knight in a jousting tournament (lines 33–7) who pulls his horse to one side, and so breaks his lance like a complete fool ('noble goose').

In contrast, Corin's descriptions of two lovers are stereotypes straight out of the world of pastoral romance:

- 'the shepherd that complained of love';
- 'the proud disdainful shepherdess'.

As you read on keep these descriptions in mind to help your thinking about different views of love portrayed in the play (see page 163).

pickpurse pickpocket
verity truthfulness, sincerity
concave hollow
covered goblet empty wineglass
tapster bartender
false reckonings untrue descriptions
much question a long conversation
traverse, athwart indirectly, across
puny tilter weak jouster
youth mounts young people get up to
remove leave here

CELIA Nay, certainly, there is no truth in him.

ROSALIND Do you think so?

CELIA Yes, I think he is not a pickpurse nor a horse-stealer but, for his verity in love, I do think him as concave as a covered goblet or a worm-eaten nut.

ROSALIND Not true in love?

CELIA Yes, when he is in; but I think he is not in.

ROSALIND You have heard him swear downright he was.

CELIA 'Was' is not 'is'; besides, the oath of a lover is no stronger than the word of a tapster: they are both the confirmers of false reckonings. He attends here in the forest on the duke your father.

ROSALIND I met the duke yesterday and had much question with him; he asked me of what parentage I was. I told him of as good as he: so he laughed and let me go. But what talk we of fathers when there is such a man as Orlando?

CELIA O that's a brave man: he writes brave verses, speaks brave words, swears brave oaths, and breaks them bravely, quite traverse, athwart the heart of his lover as a puny tilter that spurs his horse but on one side, breaks his staff like a noble goose. But all's brave that youth mounts and folly guides. – Who comes here?

Enter CORIN

CORIN Mistress and master, you have oft enquired
After the shepherd that complained of love
Who you saw sitting by me on the turf,
Praising the proud disdainful shepherdess
That was his mistress.

CELIA Well, and what of him?

CORIN If you will see a pageant truly played
Between the pale complexion of true love
And the red glow of scorn and proud disdain,
Go hence a little, and I shall conduct you
If you will mark it.

ROSALIND O come, let us remove,
The sight of lovers feedeth those in love. –
Bring us to this sight and you shall say
I'll prove a busy actor in their play.

Exeunt

Silvius begs Phebe to show him some kindness. She mocks the notion that her look might kill him. He warns that she might one day feel the pangs of love.

---

1 A third pair of lovers

Shakespeare now presents a third pair of lovers. Silvius is the love-lorn shepherd sighing vainly to his cruel mistress, the shepherdess Phebe, who scorns his love. They are Shakespeare's versions of two stock figures in the pastoral romance tradition, still very popular in his time. As you work on the scene, think how you would present Silvius and Phebe on stage, for example:

Costume and appearance: as English rustics, or like Dresden china shepherds and shepherdesses, or like Rosalind and Orlando?

Accent: they speak elaborate verse, the traditional style of high status characters. Do they have accents to match, or rural accents, or …?

2 If looks could kill (in pairs)

A convention of literary romance is that an angry glance from a lover can kill. Silvius begs Phebe not to scorn him. Even the executioner, before he strikes the fatal blow, begs the condemned man for forgiveness. Phebe taunts Silvius for his belief that she can kill him with a look. But does Silvius have a point? Talk together about whether you think that eyes have the power to wound or 'kill'.

3 Trouble ahead

Silvius' lines 27–31 warn Phebe that she may soon feel the pain of love when she is struck by Cupid's darts ('love's keen arrows'). You will shortly find that Silvius' prophecy quickly comes true.

---

dies and lives gets his living
fly thee for run from you because
'Tis pretty it's a nice idea
coward gates fearful eyelids
atomies specks of dust
counterfeit to swound pretend to swoon (faint)
rush reed, straw
cicatrice and capable impressure scar and visible impression
fresh cheek new face
power of fancy force of love

ACT 3 SCENE 6
The Forest of Arden

Enter SILVIUS and PHEBE

SILVIUS Sweet Phebe, do not scorn me, do not, Phebe.
Say that you love me not, but say not so
In bitterness. The common executioner,
Whose heart th'accustomed sight of death makes hard,
Falls not the axe upon the humbled neck
But first begs pardon. Will you sterner be
Than he that dies and lives by bloody drops?

Enter ROSALIND [*as* GANYMEDE], CELIA [*as* ALIENA], *and* CORIN [*; they stand aside*]

PHEBE I would not be thy executioner;
I fly thee for I would not injure thee.
Thou tell'st me there is murder in mine eye,
'Tis pretty, sure, and very probable
That eyes, that are the frail'st and softest things,
Who shut their coward gates on atomies,
Should be called tyrants, butchers, murderers!
Now I do frown on thee with all my heart;
And if mine eyes can wound, now let them kill thee.
Now counterfeit to swound, why, now fall down;
Or, if thou canst not, O for shame, for shame,
Lie not to say mine eyes are murderers.
Now show the wound mine eye hath made in thee.
Scratch thee but with a pin, and there remains
Some scar of it; lean upon a rush,
The cicatrice and capable impressure
Thy palm some moment keeps. But now mine eyes,
Which I have darted at thee, hurt thee not,
Nor I am sure there is no force in eyes
That can do hurt.

SILVIUS O dear Phebe,
If ever – as that 'ever' may be near –
You meet in some fresh cheek the power of fancy,
Then shall you know the wounds invisible
That love's keen arrows make.

Rosalind rebukes Phebe for having no pity for Silvius, and criticises her looks and marriage prospects. Rosalind also censures Silvius for loving Phebe. But Phebe falls in love with the disguised Rosalind.

1 'Sell when you can' (in groups of three)

Rosalind gives Phebe a dose of her own medicine, pouring scorn on her upbringing and her beauty, and urging her to marry whilst she has the chance. But Rosalind's intervention into the lovers' quarrel has an unexpected outcome: Phebe falls in love with her, thinking her to be an attractive boy, Ganymede!

In Shakespeare's time, the sexual ambiguity was heightened in performance. The audience saw a boy actor, playing a girl (Phebe), falling in love with a boy (Ganymede), who is a girl (Rosalind), played by a boy actor! Take turns to speak Rosalind's lines 35–63 using the following to help you bring out the humour and make her insults strike home:

Line 39: 'Than without candle … bed' – your looks wouldn't light up a room.

Lines 42–3: 'I see no more … sale-work' – you look like common cheap goods.

Lines 46–7: 'inky brows … eyeballs' – in Shakespeare's time, dark hair was not considered beautiful.

Line 54: ''Tis not her glass … her' – she thinks she's beautiful, not because of what she sees in the mirror, but because you tell her she is.

Line 60: 'Sell when you can … markets' – how does Rosalind deliver her most cutting insult?

exult rejoice, triumph
the wretched sad lover (Silvius)
Od's may God save
bugle glassy black
entame conquer, subdue
foggy South the south wind
properer more handsome
ill-favoured ugly
lineaments features
fasting (like a religious duty)
Foul … scoffer ugliness is made worse by scorn
chide a year together insult me for a year

PHEBE But till that time
Come not thou near me; and when, that time comes,
Afflict me with thy mocks, pity me not,
As till that time I shall not pity thee.

ROSALIND [*Coming forward*] And why, I pray you? Who might be your mother
That you insult, exult, and all at once
Over the wretched? What though you have no beauty,
As, by my faith, I see no more in you
Than without candle may go dark to bed,
Must you be therefore proud and pitiless?
Why, what means this? Why do you look on me?
I see no more in you than in the ordinary
Of Nature's sale-work – Od's my little life,
I think she means to tangle my eyes too. –
No, faith, proud mistress, hope not after it;
'Tis not your inky brows, your black silk hair,
Your bugle eyeballs, nor your cheek of cream
That can entame my spirits to your worship. –
You, foolish shepherd, wherefore do you follow her
Like foggy South, puffing with wind and rain?
You are a thousand times a properer man
Than she a woman. 'Tis such fools as you
That makes the world full of ill-favoured children.
'Tis not her glass but you that flatters her,
And out of you she sees herself more proper
Than any of her lineaments can show her. –
But, mistress, know yourself. Down on your knees,

[*Phebe kneels to Rosalind*]

And thank heaven, fasting, for a good man's love;
For I must tell you friendly in your ear,
Sell when you can: you are not for all markets.
Cry the man mercy, love him, take his offer,
Foul is most foul, being foul to be a scoffer. –
So take her to thee, shepherd; fare you well.

PHEBE Sweet youth, I pray you chide a year together;
I had rather hear you chide than this man woo.

Rosalind rejects Phebe and tells her to be kinder to Silvius. Phebe acknowledges she loves Ganymede and proposes to use Silvius as a go-between. Silvius is grateful for anything from Phebe.

---

1 To whom? (in pairs)

Rosalind has proved 'a busy actor' in the play between Silvius and Phebe. Her final two speeches are expecially 'busy', directed at different characters. As one person speaks all that Rosalind says between lines 66–79, the other says the name of the character to whom each short section is addressed. Afterwards, talk together about whether any lines might be spoken direct to the audience.

2 Christopher Marlowe – love at first sight

Phebe's lines 80–1 are probably a reference to the playwright Christopher Marlowe, who was killed in a tavern quarrel in 1593. She calls him 'Dead shepherd' and says that she now finds his wise saying ('saw') very true indeed ('of might'). The line '"Who ever loved that loved not at first sight?"' is from Marlowe's poem 'Hero and Leander'.

What are your own views on 'love at first sight'? Is it just a romantic fiction?

3 A schemer and a wimp? (in pairs)

Talk together about how far you agree with the following description:

> 'Phebe is wrapped up in herself, full of day-dreams about Ganymede/Rosalind. She barely notices Silvius, but when she does, she shows herself to be a calculating schemer because she thinks she can use his sweet love talk to achieve her own ends. Silvius is just a hapless wimp. He lets her walk all over him, seeing himself happy like the poor peasants who used to scavenge the harvest field after it had been mowed.'

---

sauce sharply taunt
vows made in wine promises made by drunkards
tuft of olives clump of olive trees
hard by nearby
ply her hard woo her vigorously
extermined destroyed
neighbourly friendly
covetousness to desire wrongly
erst was irksome used to be irritating
glean the broken ears scavenge the remaining ears of corn
scattered random

ROSALIND He's fallen in love with your foulness – [*To Silvius*] and she'll fall in love with my anger. If it be so, as fast as she answers thee with frowning looks, I'll sauce her with bitter words. – Why look you so upon me?

PHEBE For no ill will I bear you.

ROSALIND I pray you do not fall in love with me
For I am falser than vows made in wine;
Besides, I like you not. – [*To Silvius*] If you will know my house,
'Tis at the tuft of olives, here hard by. –
Will you go, sister? – Shepherd, ply her hard. –
Come, sister. – Shepherdess, look on him better
And be not proud, though all the world could see,
None could be so abused in sight as he. –
Come, to our flock. *Exeunt Rosalind, Celia, Corin*

PHEBE Dead shepherd, now I find thy saw of might:
'Who ever loved that loved not at first sight?'

SILVIUS Sweet Phebe, –

PHEBE Ha, what say'st thou, Silvius?

SILVIUS Sweet Phebe, pity me.

PHEBE Why I am sorry for thee, gentle Silvius.

SILVIUS Wherever sorrow is, relief would be.
If you do sorrow at my grief in love,
By giving love your sorrow and my grief
Were both extermined.

PHEBE Thou hast my love: is not that neighbourly?

SILVIUS I would have you.

PHEBE Why, that were covetousness.
Silvius, the time was that I hated thee,
And yet it is not that I bear thee love;
But since that thou canst talk of love so well,
Thy company, which erst was irksome to me,
I will endure – and I'll employ thee too.
But do not look for further recompense
Than thine own gladness that thou art employed.

SILVIUS So holy and so perfect is my love,
And I in such a poverty of grace
That I shall think it a most plenteous crop
To glean the broken ears after the man
That the main harvest reaps. Loose now and then
A scattered smile, and that I'll live upon.

Phebe's detailed description of Ganymede shows how much she loves him. But she denies that she does, and says she will write a taunting letter that Silvius will deliver.

---

1 Enjoy the language! (in pairs)

Phebe's speech expressing her emotional turmoil about Ganymede displays many of Shakespeare's characteristic language techniques (see pages 178–81). Use the following reminders to help you speak lines 108–34 to bring out the humour of the situation:

Antithesis: setting the word against the word. The speech is a series of oppositions: she says something, then contradicts it ('Think not I love him, though I ask for him', 'pretty'/'not very pretty', and so on).

Monosyllables: A long succession of monosyllables helps the actor to speak each word sharply and emphatically. Shakespeare gives Phebe long stretches of language full of such single-sound words. When she complains 'He said mine eyes were black, and my hair black', each monosyllabic word adds strikingly to her sense of injury.

Lists: Shakespeare loved to pile up item on item to intensify meaning and dramatic effect. The speech is a long catalogue of how Phebe has 'marked him/In parcels' (noted Ganymede feature by feature).

Repetition: the swinging rhythm of the speech is one kind of repetition. Shakespeare adds other kinds of subtle repetitions of words and phrases: 'yet', 'he'/'his', and so on.

How convincing do you find the speech as a portrayal of someone in love, but who tries to deny it?

---

erewhile just now
bounds pastures
carlot peasant, countryman
peevish irritating, foolish
proper handsome
mingled damask red and white
am remembered recall
Omittance is no quittance not replying doesn't mean I pardon him
straight immediately
passing short very sharp

PHEBE Know'st thou the youth that spoke to me erewhile?
SILVIUS Not very well; but I have met him oft
And he hath bought the cottage and the bounds
That the old carlot once was master of.
PHEBE Think not I love him, though I ask for him;
'Tis but a peevish boy – yet he talks well.
But what care I for words? Yet words do well
When he that speaks them pleases those that hear.
It is a pretty youth – not very pretty;
But sure he's proud – and yet his pride becomes him;
He'll make a proper man. The best thing in him
Is his complexion; and faster than his tongue
Did make offence, his eye did heal it up;
He is not very tall, yet for his years he's tall;
His leg is but so-so, and yet 'tis well;
There was a pretty redness in his lip,
A little riper and more lusty red
Than that mixed in his cheek: 'twas just the difference
Betwixt the constant red and mingled damask.
There be some women, Silvius, had they marked him
In parcels as I did, would have gone near
To fall in love with him: but, for my part,
I love him not nor hate him not – and yet
Have I more cause to hate him than to love him.
For what had he to do to chide at me?
He said mine eyes were black, and my hair black,
And, now I am remembered, scorned at me.
I marvel why I answered not again;
But that's all one. Omittance is no quittance.
I'll write to him a very taunting letter
And thou shalt bear it – wilt thou, Silvius?
SILVIUS Phebe, with all my heart.
PHEBE I'll write it straight:
The matter's in my head, and in my heart;
I will be bitter with him and passing short.
Go with me, Silvius.

Exeunt

Looking back at Act 3

Activities for groups or individuals

1 Bad poetry – and good

In Scene 3, Shakespeare clearly enjoys himself in writing the poetry that Orlando writes and hangs on Arden's trees. He ensures that other characters mock Orlando's awkward verses as poor poetry. But what is good poetry? Compare Orlando's efforts with Shakespeare's sonnet 18. Make a list of the differences between them, and suggest why sonnet 18 is considered to be a supreme example of poetry.

Shall I compare thee to a summer's day?
Thou art more lovely and more temperate.
Rough winds do shake the darling buds of May,
And summer's lease hath all too short a date.
Sometime too hot the eye of heaven shines,
And often is his gold complexion dimmed,
And every fair from fair sometimes declines,
By chance, or nature's changing course untrimmed.
But thy eternal summer shall not fade,
Nor lose possession of that fair thou ow'st
Nor shall Death brag thou wand'rest in his shade,
When in eternal lines to time thou grow'st.
So long as men can breathe or eyes can see,
So long lives this, and this gives life to thee.

2 Does Orlando suspect?

A convention of Shakespeare's theatre was that disguise is always effective, no one sees through it. But are there dramatic advantages if Orlando shows he is suspicious of Ganymede's gender? In Scene 3, he expresses surprise at this shepherdess' brother who speaks so wittily in a courtly accent. Talk together about what dramatic effects you might achieve in Scene 3 if Orlando suspects Ganymede is not really what 'he' seems.

3 Three pairs of lovers (see opposite)

Three pairs of lovers appear in Act 3. But what is their love like? Consider each pair and suggest how they are similar to and different from the others.

Orlando and Rosalind.

Audrey and Touchstone.

Phebe and Silvius.

Rosalind says that extremes of both melancholy or merriness are detestable. Jaques claims his melancholy is more complex than anyone else's. Rosalind mocks his pretentiousness. She ignores Orlando.

---

1 The melancholy man

Today, 'melancholy' usually means sad, depressed or morosely introverted. But it included other meanings in Shakespeare's time: serious, cynical, world-weary. Elizabethans were fascinated by what we now call neuroses or 'complexes'. They used the theory of the four humours to explain people's behaviour, personalities or moods (see page 132). Playwrights frequently put characters on stage who displayed extremes of behaviour (jealousy, anger, sadness, and so on).

Jaques is perhaps the most famous stage depiction of 'the melancholy man'. He seems to delight in his melancholy. In his conversation with Rosalind, he takes great care to fashion his image, claiming that his personality is quite different from anyone else's. But it is a melancholy pose that many Elizabethan gentlemen affected: the world-weary cynic who feels that he has seen it all.

a Rosalind's mocking farewell to Jaques reveals the affectations that these poseurs adopted: speaking in a foreign accent ('lisp'), wearing foreign clothes ('strange suits'), criticising England and seeming to hate it ('disable … nativity'), and blaming God for creating him a melancholic. How far are these the characteristics of a cynic today?

b In lines 9–13, Jaques lists different kinds of melancholy or moods: the scholar is jealous of others' achievements ('emulation'), the musician is full of imaginative creativity ('fantastical'), and so on. Are Jaques' descriptions accurate, or merely stereotypes? Suggest how you would describe the mood of a scholar, musician, courtier, soldier, lawyer, lady or lover.

---

modern censure common criticism
politic cunning
nice nit-picking
simples ingredients
sundry contemplation of various reflections on
often rumination frequent thinking
God buy you God be with you
blank verse see page 178
nativity birthplace
swam in a gondola been abroad, visited Venice

Act 4 Scene 1
The Forest of Arden

Enter ROSALIND (as GANYMEDE), and CELIA (as ALIENA)

JAQUES I prithee, pretty youth, let me be better acquainted with thee.

ROSALIND They say you are a melancholy fellow.

JAQUES I am so: I do love it better than laughing.

ROSALIND Those that are in extremity of either are abominable fellows, and betray themselves to every modern censure worse than drunkards.

JAQUES Why, 'tis good to be sad and say nothing.

ROSALIND Why then, 'tis good to be a post.

JAQUES I have neither the scholar's melancholy, which is emulation; nor the musician's, which is fantastical; nor the courtier's, which is proud; nor the soldier's, which is ambitious; nor the lawyer's, which is politic; nor the lady's, which is nice; nor the lover's, which is all these; but it is a melancholy of mine own, compounded of many simples, extracted from many objects, and indeed the sundry contemplation of my travels, in which my often rumination wraps me in a most humorous sadness.

ROSALIND A traveller! By my faith, you have great reason to be sad. I fear you have sold your own lands to see other men's. Then to have seen much and to have nothing is to have rich eyes and poor hands.

JAQUES Yes, I have gained my experience.

Enter ORLANDO

ROSALIND And your experience makes you sad. I had rather have a fool to make me merry than experience to make me sad – and to travel for it too!

ORLANDO Good day, and happiness, dear Rosalind.

JAQUES Nay then, God buy you, and you talk in blank verse!

ROSALIND Farewell, Monsieur Traveller. Look you lisp and wear strange suits; disable all the benefits of your own country; be out of love with your nativity, and almost chide God for making you that countenance you are, or I will scarce think you have swam in a gondola.

[*Exit Jaques*]

Rosalind berates Orlando for his lateness, and doubts whether he is truly in love. She jokes about deceived husbands, then demands Orlando woo her, and teases him about tongue-tied lovers.

---

1 The wooing scene (in groups of three)

Lines 31–176 are often called 'the wooing scene', in which Rosalind tricks Orlando into wooing her. He thinks he is talking to a young man, Ganymede, who has promised to act as Rosalind to cure him of his love. But it really is Rosalind, and she loves the deception!

To gain a first impression, take parts and read through to the end of the scene. Don't pause to work out things you don't understand. When you have completed your reading, work on some of the activities below and on the following pages.

a Rosalind accuses Orlando of being 'heart-whole' (not wounded by Cupid's arrow). Does she speak this and other accusations seriously or jokingly?

b 'I am in a holiday humour'. Speak lines 55–7 as if you really were in a 'holiday humour' – make the audience believe you!

c Don't worry if you have problems with lines 66–7. Everybody does. They come after Rosalind says a lover should speak before he kisses, and Orlando asks who could be lost for words ('out') in front of his mistress. Rosalind's reply could mean that if she were his mistress, he would be tongue-tied, struck dumb by her purity ('honesty') rather than by her intelligence ('wit'). But plenty of other interpretations are possible, because for Elizabethans 'ranker' could mean both 'fouler than' and 'greater than'; and both 'honesty' and 'wit' also had sexual meanings.

---

clapped him o'th'shoulder arrested him
tardy late
as lief rather
jointure marriage settlement
are fain to be beholden … wives for must thank your wives for
prevents anticipates
leer appearance, complexion
gravelled stuck (like a grounded ship)
matter things to talk about
cleanliest shift best thing to do
puts you to entreaty makes you beg
suit pleading

Why how now, Orlando, where have you been all this while? You a lover? And you serve me such another trick, never come in my sight more.

ORLANDO My fair Rosalind, I come within an hour of my promise.

ROSALIND Break an hour's promise in love? He that will divide a minute into a thousand parts and break but a part of the thousand part of a minute in the affairs of love, it may be said of him that Cupid hath clapped him o'th'shoulder, but I'll warrant him heart-whole.

ORLANDO Pardon me, dear Rosalind.

ROSALIND Nay, and you be so tardy, come no more in my sight – I had as lief be wooed of a snail.

ORLANDO Of a snail?

ROSALIND Aye, of a snail; for though he comes slowly, he carries his house on his head; a better jointure, I think, than you make a woman. Besides, he brings his destiny with him.

ORLANDO What's that?

ROSALIND Why, horns; which such as you are fain to be beholden to your wives for. But he comes armed in his fortune and prevents the slander of his wife.

ORLANDO Virtue is no horn-maker, and my Rosalind is virtuous.

ROSALIND And I am your Rosalind.

CELIA It pleases him to call you so, but he hath a Rosalind of a better leer than you.

ROSALIND Come, woo me, woo me; for now I am in a holiday humour and like enough to consent. What would you say to me now and I were your very, very Rosalind?

ORLANDO I would kiss before I spoke.

ROSALIND Nay, you were better speak first, and when you were gravelled for lack of matter you might take occasion to kiss. Very good orators when they are out, they will spit, and for lovers, lacking – God warrant us – matter, the cleanliest shift is to kiss.

ORLANDO How if the kiss be denied?

ROSALIND Then she puts you to entreaty, and there begins new matter.

ORLANDO Who could be out, being before his beloved mistress?

ROSALIND Marry, that should you if I were your mistress, or I should think my honesty ranker than my wit.

ORLANDO What, of my suit?

ROSALIND Not out of your apparel, and yet out of your suit. Am not I your Rosalind?

Orlando claims that he will die for love. Rosalind lampoons his claim, telling of famous lovers who died – but not for love. She asks Celia to act as priest and marry her to Orlando.

From left to right: Rosalind, Celia, Orlando. Find a line from the script opposite as a suitable caption for this picture.

attorney proxy (someone who acts for you)
videlicet namely
Troilus in classical mythology, a Trojan prince who loved the Greek Cressida (he was killed by Achilles)
Leander in Greek mythology, he loved Hero and swam the Hellespont each night to visit her. He drowned in a storm
found it was blamed it on
of this mind think like this
Fridays and Saturdays days of fasting
Go to stop it

ORLANDO I take some joy to say you are, because I would be talking of her.

ROSALIND Well, in her person, I say I will not have you.

ORLANDO Then, in mine own person, I die.

ROSALIND No, faith, die by attorney. The poor world is almost six thousand years old and in all this time there was not any man died in his own person, videlicet, in a love-cause. Troilus had his brains dashed out with a Grecian club, yet he did what he could to die before, and he is one of the patterns of love; Leander, he would have lived many a fair year though Hero had turned nun, if it had not been for a hot midsummer night, for, good youth, he went but forth to wash him in the Hellespont and, being taken with the cramp, was drowned, and the foolish chroniclers of that age found it was Hero of Sestos. But these are all lies: men have died from time to time – and worms have eaten them – but not for love.

ORLANDO I would not have my right Rosalind of this mind, for I protest her frown might kill me.

ROSALIND By this hand, it will not kill a fly. But come, now I will be your Rosalind in a more coming-on disposition and, ask me what you will, I will grant it.

ORLANDO Then love me, Rosalind.

ROSALIND Yes, faith, will I, Fridays and Saturdays and all.

ORLANDO And wilt thou have me?

ROSALIND Aye, and twenty such.

ORLANDO What sayest thou?

ROSALIND Are you not good?

ORLANDO I hope so.

ROSALIND Why then, can one desire too much of a good thing? – Come, sister, you shall be the priest and marry us. – Give me your hand, Orlando. – What do you say, sister?

ORLANDO Pray thee marry us.

CELIA I cannot say the words.

ROSALIND You must begin: 'Will you, Orlando – '

CELIA Go to. – Will you, Orlando, have to wife this Rosalind?

ORLANDO I will.

ROSALIND Aye, but when?

ORLANDO Why, now, as fast as she can marry us.

ROSALIND Then you must say, 'I take thee, Rosalind, for wife.'

ORLANDO I take thee, Rosalind, for wife.

Rosalind jokes at her own forwardness, then comments on how time sours marriages. She warns of her future giddy behaviour and hints that wives and husbands are unfaithful. She criticises Orlando's proposed absence.

1 Rosalind in critical mode (in pairs)

Find suitable tones and styles for how Rosalind delivers her various criticisms, changing her mood to suit each one.

Lines 111–12: criticises herself for being too hasty in speaking her marriage vow before the 'priest' speaks it.

Lines 117–19: criticises husbands for becoming as bleak and cold as December when they are married – and wives change too.

Lines 129–39: criticises women for chattering too much and for being unfaithful – just as husbands are. There may be a sexual joke running through the lines (in Shakespeare's time 'wit' had sexual meanings).

Lines 140–1: criticises a wife who cannot blame her husband for her own faults ('cannot … her husband's occasion'). Such a wife will raise foolish children.

Lines 146–9: criticises Orlando for leaving, saying he thinks little of her: she is just a woman rejected ('but one cast away').

2 This is what I'll do! (in pairs)

In lines 119–25, Rosalind lists how she will behave when she is married, ranging from violent jealousy to laughing like a hyena. Invent actions to show each behaviour she lists.

commission authority
goes before speaks before
Barbary cock-pigeon fiercely protective male pigeon
new-fangled amused by novelties
Diana … fountain in Roman mythology, the goddess of chastity in floods of tears
waywarder more fickle
casement window
'Wit, whither wilt' stop talking (an Elizabethan catch-phrase)
check rebuke

ROSALIND I might ask you for your commission, but I do take thee, Orlando, for my husband. There's a girl goes before the priest, and certainly a woman's thought runs before her actions.

ORLANDO So do all thoughts: they are winged.

ROSALIND Now, tell me how long you would have her after you have possessed her?

ORLANDO For ever and a day.

ROSALIND Say a day without the 'ever'. No, no, Orlando: men are April when they woo, December when they wed; maids are May when they are maids, but the sky changes when they are wives. I will be more jealous of thee than a Barbary cock-pigeon over his hen; more clamorous than a parrot against rain, more new-fangled than an ape; more giddy in my desires than a monkey. I will weep for nothing, like Diana in the fountain, and I will do that when you are disposed to be merry. I will laugh like a hyena, and that when thou art inclined to sleep.

ORLANDO But will my Rosalind do so?

ROSALIND By my life, she will do as I do.

ORLANDO O, but she is wise.

ROSALIND Or else she could not have the wit to do this: the wiser, the waywarder. Make the doors upon a woman's wit, and it will out at the casement; shut that, and 'twill out at the key hole; stop that, 'twill fly with the smoke out at the chimney.

ORLANDO A man that had a wife with such a wit, he might say, 'Wit, whither wilt?'

ROSALIND Nay, you might keep that check for it till you met your wife's wit going to your neighbour's bed.

ORLANDO And what wit could wit have to excuse that?

ROSALIND Marry, to say she came to seek you there: you shall never take her without her answer unless you take her without her tongue. O, that woman that cannot make her fault her husband's occasion, let her never nurse her child herself for she will breed it like a fool.

ORLANDO For these two hours, Rosalind, I will leave thee.

ROSALIND Alas, dear love, I cannot lack thee two hours.

ORLANDO I must attend the duke at dinner, by two o'clock I will be with thee again.

ROSALIND Aye, go your ways, go your ways. I knew what you would prove – my friends told me as much, and I thought no less. That flattering tongue of yours won me. 'Tis but one cast away, and so come, Death! Two o'clock is your hour?

Rosalind warns Orlando not to be late. Celia rebukes Rosalind for her criticism of women, but Rosalind declares she is immeasurably deeply in love. Celia remains sceptical.

---

1 Rosalind's changing moods (in pairs)

Check quickly through this scene to identify all of Rosalind's moods. Find a way to display them visually.

2 Is Celia genuinely upset? (in pairs)

In the early scenes of the play, Celia had quite a large speaking role. Now, as Rosalind plays her love scenes with Orlando, Celia has less and less to say. She was silent in Act 3 Scene 6, and here only gets the chance (reluctantly?) to act as 'priest' to 'marry' the lovers. At the scene's end, she has only six lines to express her feelings.

Celia criticises Rosalind for what she has said about women ('misused our sex'), and adapts the proverb 'It is the foul bird that defiles its own nest' (only bad women criticise women). When Rosalind tells of her deep love, Celia tartly remarks that her love runs out as fast as it runs in. To Rosalind's desire to find a shady spot to sigh for Orlando, Celia merely says 'And I'll sleep'.

Celia has a variety of possible ways to play this final episode. Is she exasperated, or does she speak good-humouredly, using a mocking style that conceals genuine affection? Or is she genuinely angry and disconsolate, devastated at the thought that her former close relationship with Rosalind has ended?

Take parts as Celia and Rosalind and play lines 162–76 to explore different versions of Celia's feelings (exasperated, joking, genuinely annoyed, and so on). Does Rosalind listen to Celia at all, or is she solely caught up with her own emotions?

---

in good earnest seriously
pretty oaths … dangerous lovers' oaths
gross band huge group
censure criticism
try judge
love-prate prattle about love
many fathom deep infinitely, drowned
sounded measured (in fathoms)
bastard of Venus Cupid
begot of thought fathered in sadness
spleen passion

ORLANDO Aye, sweet Rosalind.

ROSALIND By my troth, and in good earnest, and so God mend me, and by all pretty oaths that are not dangerous, if you break one jot of your promise or come one minute behind your hour, I will think you the most pathetical break-promise, and the most hollow lover, and the most unworthy of her you call Rosalind that may be chosen out of the gross band of the unfaithful. Therefore beware my censure, and keep your promise.

ORLANDO With no less religion than if thou wert indeed my Rosalind. So adieu.

ROSALIND Well, Time is the old justice that examines all such offenders, and let Time try. Adieu.

Exit [*Orlando*]

CELIA You have simply misused our sex in your love-prate. We must have your doublet and hose plucked over your head, and show the world what the bird hath done to her own nest.

ROSALIND O coz, coz, coz, my pretty little coz, that thou didst know how many fathom deep I am in love! But it cannot be sounded: my affection hath an unknown bottom, like the Bay of Portugal.

CELIA Or rather bottomless, that as fast as you pour affection in, it runs out.

ROSALIND No, that same wicked bastard of Venus that was begot of thought, conceived of spleen, and born of madness, that blind rascally boy that abuses everyone's eyes because his own are out, let him be judge how deep I am in love. I'll tell thee, Aliena, I cannot be out of the sight of Orlando. I'll go find a shadow and sigh till he come.

CELIA And I'll sleep.

Exeunt

Jaques proposes that the lord who killed the deer be presented in triumph to Duke Senior. The lords' song claims that it is man's destiny to be a cuckold.

1 How would you present the scene?

The scene has been played in all kinds of ways: as a celebration of hunting, as a festival of forest life, as Celia's dream of Rosalind being hunted (Celia stayed on stage), as a very bloody pagan ritual. Between 1879 and 1919, productions of *As You Like It* at Stratford-upon-Avon brought on stage a stuffed deer from the herd at nearby Charlecote Park (where Shakespeare is rumoured to have poached deer). Work out your own staging of Scene 2.

branch of victory victory wreath
The rest shall bear this bourdon all men's destiny is to endure being cuckolds; let everyone carry the dead deer; everybody join in the chorus

Take thou no scorn to wear the horn don't disdain to be a cuckold
crest ere thou wast born destiny before you were born
laugh to scorn mock, ridicule

Act 4 Scene 2
A glade in the Forest of Arden

Enter JAQUES and LORDS, FORESTERS bearing the antlers and skin of a deer

JAQUES Which is he that killed the deer?

FIRST LORD Sir, it was I.

JAQUES Let's present him to the duke like a Roman conqueror – and it would do well to set the deer's horns upon his head for a branch of victory. – Have you no song, forester, for this purpose?

FIRST FORESTER Yes, sir.

JAQUES Sing it. 'Tis no matter how it be in tune, so it make noise enough.

Music
Song

LORDS What shall he have that killed the deer?
His leather skin and horns to wear.
Then sing him home,
The rest shall bear this bourdon.

Take thou no scorn to wear the horn,
It was a crest ere thou wast born;
Thy father's father wore it,
And thy father bore it;
The horn, the horn, the lusty horn,
Is not a thing to laugh to scorn.

Exeunt

Celia mocks Rosalind's impatience that Orlando is late. Silvius tells that Phebe's letter contains an angry message. Rosalind seems annoyed and criticises Phebe.

---

1 Intended to hurt?

Rosalind is annoyed that Orlando has not come as he promised. Celia suggests he has gone to hunt in the forest, and adds the mocking comment that he has fallen asleep. Are Celia's comments barbed, intended to hurt? Advise Celia how to speak lines 3–4.

2 'Pardon me …'

Silvius' 'Pardon me,/I am but as a guiltless messenger', spoken with an air of wide-eyed innocence, often gets a big laugh in the theatre. How would you speak his apology?

3 Exotic Arden

Phebe's letter says that she could not love Ganymede if he were the only man in the world ('as rare as phoenix'). The phoenix was a mythical bird. Only one was believed to be alive at any time. After 500 years it died, but was born again in fire. You can find more on page 173 about how Shakespeare builds up the impression of the Forest of Arden as a mysterious place full of all kinds of wonders.

4 Why is Rosalind so critical?

After reading the letter, Rosalind calls Silvius a fool, and launches an attack on Phebe. But why? As you will shortly discover, the letter is quite different from how Silvius and Rosalind describe it opposite. So why is Rosalind critical of both the messenger and the writer? Keep the question in mind as you read on.

---

warrant you guarantee that
waspish action fierce movements
tenor message
play the swaggerer fight back
bear all endure everything
fair handsome
Od's God save
not the hare that I do hunt I don't seek her love
device invention
freestone-coloured sandy yellow
hussif's housewife's

ACT 4 SCENE 3
The Forest of Arden

Enter ROSALIND (as GANYMEDE) and CELIA (as ALIENA)

ROSALIND How say you now, is it not past two o'clock? And here much Orlando!

CELIA I warrant you, with pure love and troubled brain he hath ta'en his bow and arrows and is gone forth – to sleep. Look who comes here.

Enter SILVIUS [*with a letter*]

SILVIUS My errand is to you, fair youth.
My gentle Phebe did bid me give you this:
I know not the contents but, as I guess
By the stern brow and waspish action
Which she did use as she was writing of it,
It bears an angry tenor. Pardon me,
I am but as a guiltless messenger.

ROSALIND [*After reading the letter*] Patience herself would startle at this letter
And play the swaggerer: bear this, bear all.
She says I am not fair, that I lack manners;
She calls me proud, and that she could not love me
Were man as rare as phoenix. Od's my will,
Her love is not the hare that I do hunt –
Why writes she so to me? Well, shepherd, well?
This is a letter of your own device.

SILVIUS No, I protest, I know not the contents;
Phebe did write it.

ROSALIND Come, come, you are a fool
And turned into the extremity of love.
I saw her hand, she has a leathern hand,
A freestone-coloured hand. (I verily did think
That her old gloves were on, but 'twas her hands.)
She has a hussif's hand – but that's no matter.
I say she never did invent this letter:
This is a man's invention and his hand.

SILVIUS Sure, it is hers.

Rosalind claims that Phebe's letter is full of insults. But when she reads the letter, it reveals that Phebe is passionately in love with Ganymede and wants him to send a secret reply by Silvius.

---

1 Silvius' reaction (in pairs)

Rosalind builds up a picture of the fierce and insulting content of Phebe's letter. Silvius wants to hear it. When Rosalind reads, the letter turns out quite different from what Silvius expected. It describes Ganymede as a god become man who has conquered Phebe's heart. Phebe begs for a reply in a sealed letter from Ganymede, and Silvius is to deliver it.

What is the effect of this revelation on Silvius? Take parts and act out lines 30–62, to show Silvius' reactions to the letter.

2 Politically incorrect (in pairs)

Step into role as director and actor. The actor wants to cut lines 34–5 on the grounds they are offensive. The director wants to keep the lines, arguing that to Elizabethans, Ethiopians and black faces were the symbols of evil, and the lines only show the beliefs of Shakespeare's time. Argue your case.

3 Shakespeare creates words

Shakespeare loved making up words:

Line 33: 'giant-rude' (immensely insulting). Use the hyphen to invent some similar compound words of your own, for example, alligator-hungry, dragon-scary, and so on.

Line 38: 'She Phebes me' (she insults me in her own typical style). Invent a few similar phrases, using someone's name as a verb.

---

boisterous bragging, quarrelsome
challengers duellists, opponents
Turk to Christian (traditional enemies)
rail scold, insult
godhead laid apart divinity put aside (and become man)
Warr'st thou why do you make war
in mild aspect gentle looks
chid rebuked
seal up thy mind send a sealed letter
kind nature

ROSALIND Why, a boisterous and a cruel style,
A style for challengers. Why, she defies me
Like Turk to Christian. Woman's gentle brain
Could not drop forth such giant-rude invention,
Such Ethiop words, blacker in their effect
Than in their countenance. Will you hear the letter?
SILVIUS So please you, for I never heard it yet,
Yet heard too much of Phebe's cruelty.
ROSALIND She Phebes me. Mark how the tyrant writes:
Reads 'Art thou god to shepherd turned,
That a maiden's heart hath burned?'
Can a woman rail thus?
SILVIUS Call you this railing?
ROSALIND *Reads* 'Why, thy godhead laid apart,
Warr'st thou with a woman's heart?' –
Did you ever hear such railing? –
'Whiles the eye of man did woo me,
That could do no vengeance to me.' –
Meaning me a beast!
'If the scorn of your bright eyne
Have power to raise such love in mine,
Alack, in me what strange effect
Would they work in mild aspect?
Whiles you chid me, I did love;
How then might your prayers move?
He that brings this love to thee
Little knows this love in me;
And by him seal up thy mind,
Whether that thy youth and kind
Will the faithful offer take
Of me and all that I can make,
Or else by him my love deny,
And then I'll study how to die.'
SILVIUS Call you this chiding?
CELIA Alas, poor shepherd.

Rosalind rebukes Silvius for being made so feeble by love. Oliver recognises Celia and Ganymede, and brings a bloody handkerchief from Orlando. He begins his story.

---

1 Does Silvius deserve it?

Celia expresses pity for Silvius, but Rosalind scorns him for loving Phebe who has made such a fool of him. What is your own attitude to Silvius? Does he deserve such harsh treatment, both from the woman he loves, and from Rosalind? If you were acting Silvius, what response would you hope to evoke from the audience throughout lines 63–9? Describe how you would act to produce that response.

2 Enter Oliver

Oliver, Orlando's wicked brother, was last seen in Act 3 Scene 1 being manhandled by Duke Frederick's officers. He was despatched to capture Orlando, dead or alive. Now he seems a changed man, greeting the princesses courteously, and bringing news of Orlando.

As you will shortly discover, Oliver and Celia fall in love at first sight. Does their language opposite give any suggestion of that instant falling in love? Suggest how you would stage lines 70–85 to give the audience the first hint of their mutual attraction.

3 'This bloody napkin'

Oliver produces a bloodstained handkerchief. Before you turn the page, make a guess about the part it will play in the story.

4 'Chewing the food of sweet and bitter fancy'

Line 96 describes Orlando's thoughts as he wandered through the forest. One possible meaning is 'turning good and bad memories over in his mind'. Suggest another way of expressing the image.

---

false strains deceitful tunes (tricks)
tame snake harmless worm
entreat beg
purlieus borders
neighbour bottom nearby valley
rank of osiers row of willows
an eye … description I can recognise you by what I've been told
bestows himself behaves, appears
fancy love
Lo what befell listen to what happened

ROSALIND Do you pity him? No, he deserves no pity. – Wilt thou love such a woman? What, to make thee an instrument and play false strains upon thee? Not to be endured! Well, go your way to her – for I see love hath made thee a tame snake – and say this to her: that if she love me, I charge her to love thee; if she will not, I will never have her, unless thou entreat for her. If you be a true lover, hence, and not a word; for here comes more company.

Exit Silvius

Enter OLIVER

OLIVER Good morrow, fair ones. Pray you, if you know
Where in the purlieus of this forest stands
A sheepcote fenced about with olive-trees.
CELIA West of this place, down in the neighbour bottom;
The rank of osiers by the murmuring stream,
Left on your right hand, brings you to the place.
But at this hour the house doth keep itself:
There's none within.
OLIVER If that an eye may profit by a tongue,
Then should I know you by description:
Such garments, and such years. 'The boy is fair,
Of female favour, and bestows himself
Like a ripe sister; the woman low
And browner than her brother.' Are not you
The owner of the house I did enquire for?
CELIA It is no boast, being asked, to say we are.
OLIVER Orlando doth commend him to you both,
And to that youth he calls his Rosalind
He sends this bloody napkin. Are you he?
ROSALIND I am. What must we understand by this?
OLIVER Some of my shame, if you will know of me
What man I am, and how, and why, and where
This handkerchief was stained.
CELIA I pray you tell it.
OLIVER When last the young Orlando parted from you,
He left a promise to return again
Within an hour and, pacing through the forest,
Chewing the food of sweet and bitter fancy,
Lo what befell. He threw his eye aside
And mark what object did present itself.

Oliver relates how Orlando saw an unkempt sleeping man threatened by a snake and lion. Orlando recognised the man as his brother, and killed the lion. Oliver reveals he was the sleeping man.

---

1 Oliver's story (in groups of three)

The story Oliver tells is improbably melodramatic. It is an example of the conventions of literary pastoral, in which forests can contain snakes and lions and all kinds of exotic animals and events. Work out how you would deliver Oliver's story on stage, and how the two women react. Use the following points to help your preparation:

- To whom does Oliver tell his story: to Celia, to Rosalind, or to both? Remember he's fallen in love with Celia.
- Block the episode to show how the three characters stand, sit or move in relation to each other.
- How does Celia behave when Oliver reveals his identity?
- Does Oliver listen to Rosalind, or is he fully caught up with Celia?
- Do you think the snake and the lion have symbolic significance, for example, as images of deceit and brutality, or as …?

2 Moral dilemma

Oliver's story is a tale of forgiveness and reconciliation, telling how brotherly love triumphed over the unnaturalness of brotherly hate. Give your reaction to the following comment:

> 'This is the heart of the moral dimension of the play. Orlando sees the brother, who has treated him so cruelly, about to be killed by a lion. What should he do? Twice he turned away, leaving his brother to the mercy of the lion. But finally "kindness" and "nature" overcame any feeling of resentment and revenge, and he risked his own life to save his brother.'

---

dry antiquity old age
gilded golden
indented glides zigzag movements
couching crouching
disposition nature
render describe
unnatural cruel, unkind
just occasion legitimate opportunity
hurtling violent struggle
contrive plot
conversion change to goodness

Under an old oak whose boughs were mossed with age,
And high top bald with dry antiquity,
A wretched ragged man, o'ergrown with hair,
Lay sleeping on his back; about his neck
A green and gilded snake had wreathed itself,
Who, with her head, nimble in threats, approached
The opening of his mouth. But suddenly
Seeing Orlando, it unlinked itself
And with indented glides did slip away
Into a bush; under which bush's shade
A lioness, with udders all drawn dry,
Lay couching head on ground, with cat-like watch
When that the sleeping man should stir – for 'tis
The royal disposition of that beast
To prey on nothing that doth seem as dead.
This seen, Orlando did approach the man
And found it was his brother, his elder brother.

CELIA O, I have heard him speak of that same brother,
And he did render him the most unnatural
That lived amongst men.

OLIVER And well he might so do,
For well I know he was unnatural.

ROSALIND But to Orlando – did he leave him there,
Food to the sucked and hungry lioness?

OLIVER Twice did he turn his back and purposed so.
But kindness, nobler ever than revenge,
And nature, stronger than his just occasion,
Made him give battle to the lioness,
Who quickly fell before him; in which hurtling
From miserable slumber I awaked.

CELIA Are you his brother?

ROSALIND Was't you he rescued?

CELIA Was't you that did so oft contrive to kill him?

OLIVER 'Twas I, but 'tis not I. I do not shame
To tell you what I was, since my conversion
So sweetly tastes, being the thing I am.

ROSALIND But for the bloody napkin?

Oliver relates how Orlando fainted, then recovered and sent Oliver with the bloodstained handkerchief to Rosalind. She faints, recovers, and pretends her swooning is a pretence.

1 Ganymede or Rosalind? (in groups of three)

The final moments of Scene 3 are rich in comic possibilities. Rosalind is desperate to learn the meaning of the bloodstained handkerchief, and for news of Orlando. But Oliver makes her wait ('By and by'). Some critics think that Oliver is totally caught up with Celia, with whom he has fallen in love. Others are confident that Oliver sees through Rosalind's disguise as Ganymede.

Talk together about the different dramatic effects that can be achieved if Oliver knows, suspects, or does not know that Ganymede is really Rosalind in disguise. Then take parts and play the lines opposite to explore different possibilities.

Make your first version one in which Oliver is completely unsuspecting of Ganymede's gender. Then try out a version in which Oliver strongly suspects that Ganymede is Rosalind. Use the following questions to guide your presentation:

a How does Rosalind behave throughout Oliver's story?

b Does Oliver begin to suspect that Ganymede is not a boy when he carries out the stage direction *Raising Rosalind* at line 155?

c At what moments does Rosalind seem close to giving herself away? When she hears that Orlando called out her name (line 144)? When she exclaims 'I would I were at home'? Or …?

d Does Celia give the game away? Trying to revive Rosalind, she calls her 'Cousin' at line 154.

e How might Oliver behave if he simply isn't sure, but suspects that something odd is going on?

By and by in a moment
recountments stories
array clothes
entertainment hospitality
small space short time
in sport playfully
a body anybody
counterfeited faked, imitated
testimony evidence
passion of earnest genuine emotion
devise work out

OLIVER By and by.
When from the first to last betwixt us two,
Tears our recountments had most kindly bathed –
As how I came into that desert place –
In brief, he led me to the gentle duke
Who gave me fresh array and entertainment,
Committing me unto my brother's love,
Who led me instantly unto his cave;
There stripped himself and here, upon his arm,
The lioness had torn some flesh away,
Which all this while had bled; and now he fainted,
And cried in fainting upon Rosalind.
Brief, I recovered him, bound up his wound,
And, after some small space, being strong at heart,
He sent me hither, stranger as I am,
To tell this story that you might excuse
His broken promise, and to give this napkin,
Dyed in this blood, unto the shepherd youth
That he in sport doth call his Rosalind.
[*Rosalind faints*]

CELIA Why, how now? Ganymede, sweet Ganymede!

OLIVER Many will swoon when they do look on blood.

CELIA There is more in it. – Cousin! Ganymede!

OLIVER [*Raising Rosalind*] Look, he recovers.

ROSALIND I would I were at home.

CELIA We'll lead you thither. – I pray you, will you take him by the arm.

OLIVER Be of good cheer, youth. You a man? You lack a man's heart.

ROSALIND I do so, I confess it. Ah, sirrah, a body would think this was well counterfeited. I pray you tell your brother how well I counterfeited. Heigh-ho!

OLIVER This was not counterfeit: there is too great testimony in your complexion that it was a passion of earnest.

ROSALIND Counterfeit, I assure you.

OLIVER Well then, take a good heart, and counterfeit to be a man.

ROSALIND So I do. But, i'faith, I should have been a woman by right.

CELIA Come, you look paler and paler: pray you, draw homewards. – Good, sir, go with us.

OLIVER That will I. For I must bear answer back how you excuse my brother, Rosalind.

ROSALIND I shall devise something. But I pray you commend my counterfeiting to him. Will you go? *Exeunt*

Looking back at Act 4

Activities for groups or individuals

1 Jaques' melancholy – the four humours

In Scene 1, Jaques declares that he has his own, very special melancholy. A popular belief in Shakespeare's time was that personality was determined by four 'humours' (fluids in the human body). These were blood (producing bravery), phlegm (producing calmness), 'yellowe' (producing anger), and black bile (producing melancholy). The belief was that if the four humours were in balance, the result was a healthy and temperate person. But if one humour dominated, the outcome was an unbalanced personality. Many Elizabethans would think that Jaques, with his extreme melancholy, had an excess of black bile.

Do you think the theory of humours has any validity today? For example, does it apply in any way to your temperament?

2 Stag hunting

Work with a partner, each of you stepping into role as a director. One of you is very anti-hunting, the other favours it or is tolerant of it. Argue your case for how you would stage Scene 2 portraying the end of the hunt.

3 Write Oliver's ballad

Remind yourself of the story Oliver tells in Scene 3. Compose a ballad that tells his tale. It explains how he came to the forest, and why he has changed from the wicked brother he once was.

4 Rosalind's mood changes

Rosalind experiences violent swings of emotion in Scenes 1 and 3. Find a way of presenting her shifts of mood, perhaps as a graph, or as a series of tableaux, each accompanied with a brief narration.

5 Celia's silence

After Act 4, Celia does not speak again in the play. Why should she remain silent? Write her diary entry that describes what she did and what she felt and thought throughout Act 4.

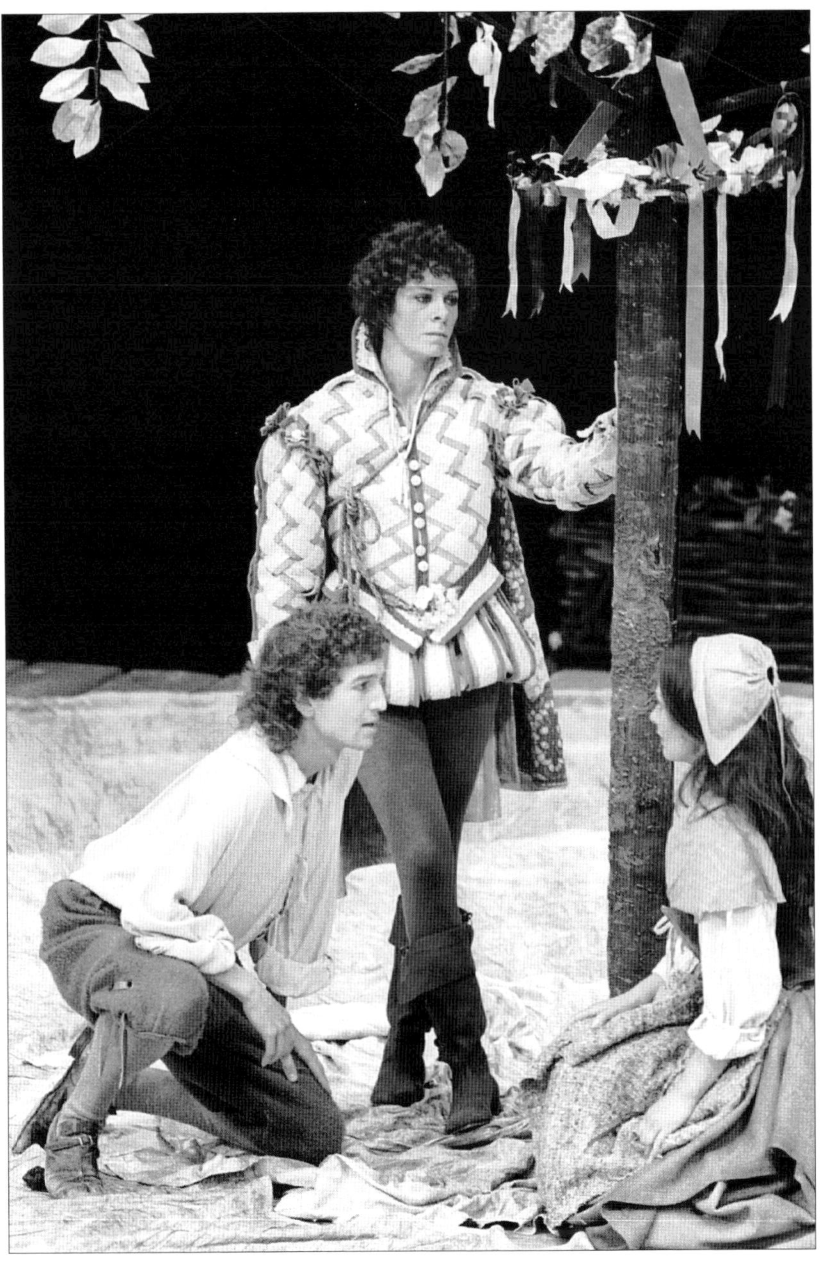

As You Like It is much concerned with mistaken identity. In this picture, the lovers are Silvius and Phebe from a moment in Act 3 Scene 6. Suggest several reasons why they could easily be taken for Oliver and Celia in Act 4 Scene 3.

Audrey regrets that Sir Oliver Martext did not marry her to Touchstone. She denies that William has any claim on her. William enters, and Touchstone begins to mock him.

Another lover appears in the play, but William seems no real opponent for Touchstone in winning Audrey.

old gentleman Jaques
lays claim to wants to marry
interest in claim on
clown country bumpkin
troth truth, faith
flouting mocking

we cannot hold we can't help doing it
Good ev'n good evening
so-so average

Act 5 Scene 1
The Forest of Arden

Enter TOUCHSTONE and AUDREY

TOUCHSTONE We shall find a time, Audrey; patience, gentle Audrey.

AUDREY Faith, the priest was good enough, for all the old gentleman's saying.

TOUCHSTONE A most wicked Sir Oliver, Audrey, a most vile Martext. But, Audrey, there is a youth here in the forest lays claim to you.

AUDREY Aye, I know who 'tis. He hath no interest in me in the world.

Enter WILLIAM

Here comes the man you mean.

TOUCHSTONE It is meat and drink to me to see a clown. By my troth, we that have good wits have much to answer for. We shall be flouting; we cannot hold.

WILLIAM Good ev'n, Audrey.

AUDREY God ye good ev'n, William.

WILLIAM [*Taking off his hat*] And good ev'n to you, sir.

TOUCHSTONE Good ev'n, gentle friend. Cover thy head, cover thy head. Nay prithee, be covered. How old are you, friend?

WILLIAM Five and twenty, sir.

TOUCHSTONE A ripe age. Is thy name William?

WILLIAM William, sir.

TOUCHSTONE A fair name. Wast born i'th'forest here?

WILLIAM Aye, sir, I thank God.

TOUCHSTONE 'Thank God': a good answer. Art rich?

WILLIAM Faith, sir, so-so.

TOUCHSTONE 'So-so' is good, very good, very excellent good – and yet it is not: it is but so-so. Art thou wise?

WILLIAM Aye, sir, I have a pretty wit.

TOUCHSTONE Why, thou say'st well. I do now remember a saying: 'The fool doth think he is wise, but the wise man knows himself to be a fool.'

Touchstone bamboozles William with impressive-sounding but empty language. He says that he, not William, must marry Audrey, and threatens William with all kinds of punishments.

1 **Act out the scene** (in groups of three)

In Scene 1, Touchstone talks a good deal of high-flown nonsense in order to get the better of William. He contemptuously refers to ordinary language as 'the vulgar', 'the boorish', 'the common'. When Touchstone talks of 'The heathen philosopher' he is probably just making up a non-existent but important sounding figure to scare off William (who may be standing wide-eyed and open-mouthed – which provokes Touchstone's remark).

The encounter is another example of the conflict between court (Touchstone) and country (William), with Touchstone determined to show the superiority of the court. But in one production, as Touchstone finished his threats, William seized him and almost strangled him until Audrey pleaded 'Do, good William'.

Take parts and act out the whole scene. Think especially about how you want the audience to feel towards William.

2 **William's dramatic function** (in pairs)

Why did Shakespeare invent William? Step into role as Touchstone, who has become a university professor. Use elaborate language to argue for each of the following possibilities:

- a private joke on Shakespeare's own name;
- to provide yet another view of love;
- to make a contrast with the previous scene;
- just for fun.

---

figure in rhetoric saying in the book of speech-making
'*ipse*' he himself (Latin)
to wit that is to say
bastinado beating with a stick
steel sword fighting
bandy with thee in faction compete in exchanging insults with you
policy deceitful scheming
Trip skip, look lively!

[*William gapes*]

The heathen philosopher, when he had a desire to eat a grape, would open his lips when he put it into his mouth, meaning thereby that grapes were made to eat and lips to open. You do love this maid?

WILLIAM I do, sir.

TOUCHSTONE Give me your hand. Art thou learned?

WILLIAM No, sir.

TOUCHSTONE Then learn this of me: to have is to have. For it is a figure in rhetoric that drink, being poured out of a cup into a glass, by filling the one doth empty the other. For all your writers do consent that '*ipse*' is he. Now you are not *ipse*, for I am he.

WILLIAM Which he, sir?

TOUCHSTONE He, sir, that must marry this woman. Therefore, you clown, abandon, which is in the vulgar, 'leave the society', which in the boorish is 'company', of this female, which in the common is 'woman': which together is 'abandon the society of this female'; or, clown, thou perishest or, to they better understanding, 'diest', or, to wit, 'I kill thee', 'make thee away', 'translate thy life into death, thy liberty into bondage'! I will deal in poison with thee, or in bastinado, or in steel! I will bandy with thee in faction, I will o'errun thee with policy – I will kill thee a hundred and fifty ways! Therefore, tremble and depart.

AUDREY Do, good William.

WILLIAM God rest you merry, sir.

Exit

Enter CORIN

CORIN Our master and mistress seeks you. Come away, away.

TOUCHSTONE Trip, Audrey, trip, Audrey. – I attend, I attend.

Exeunt

Oliver confirms that he instantly fell in love with Celia. He promises to give Orlando all his inheritance. Rosalind describes how Oliver and Celia fell in love at first sight and now long for marriage.

---

1 The speed of love, the speed of speech? (in pairs)

Shakespeare's theme on the opposite page is the speed of love. He provides Orlando, Oliver and Rosalind with a language style that matches the rapidity of falling in love at first sight. All three have speeches that pile item on item, event on event, in rapid succession.

For example, Rosalind begins with two examples of speed: how two rams rush at each other in a fight, and how Julius Caesar boasted of a rapid victory, saying 'I came, saw, and overcame' (I came, I saw, I conquered). She then describes the development of Oliver and Celia's love as a rapid procession of steps.

Experiment with ways of speaking the three speeches (lines 1–9 and lines 23–32). Do you think they should be spoken as quickly as possible, or with distinct pauses between each section, or in some other way?

2 Does Orlando know Ganymede is Rosalind?

Oliver greets Rosalind as 'fair sister' (line 13), and Orlando says that his brother told him of 'greater wonders' than how Ganymede pretended to faint ('counterfeited to sound'). Rosalind replies she knows what he means ('I know where you are') and says it is about Oliver's and Celia's love at first sight. But is Rosalind just trying to cover up that Orlando now sees through her disguise as Ganymede?

As you read on, keep thinking about the different ways Orlando would behave if he knows the truth, or if he still believes that Ganymede is a boy.

---

grant agree to marry you
persevere continue
giddiness suddenness
revenue income
estate upon settle on, give to
all's contented followers all his happy courtiers
thrasonical boastful
degrees steps
incontinent immediately (line 30), sexually active (line 31)
wrath passion

Act 5 Scene 2
The Forest of Arden

Enter ORLANDO and OLIVER

ORLANDO Is't possible that on so little acquaintance you should like her, that, but seeing, you should love her, and, loving, woo, and, wooing, she should grant? And will you persevere to enjoy her?

OLIVER Neither call the giddiness of it in question; the poverty of her, the small acquaintance, my sudden wooing, nor her sudden consenting. But say with me, I love Aliena; say with her that she loves me; consent with both, that we may enjoy each other. It shall be to your good, for my father's house and all the revenue that was old Sir Roland's will I estate upon you, and here live and die a shepherd.

Enter ROSALIND [*as* GANYMEDE]

ORLANDO You have my consent. Let your wedding be tomorrow; thither will I invite the duke and all's contented followers. Go you, and prepare Aliena, for look you, here comes my 'Rosalind'.

ROSALIND God save you, brother.

OLIVER And you, fair sister. [*Exit*]

ROSALIND O, my dear Orlando, how it grieves me to see thee wear thy heart in a scarf.

ORLANDO It is my arm.

ROSALIND I thought thy heart had been wounded with the claws of a lion.

ORLANDO Wounded it is, but with the eyes of a lady.

ROSALIND Did your brother tell you how I counterfeited to sound when he showed me your handkerchief?

ORLANDO Aye, and greater wonders than that.

ROSALIND O, I know where you are. Nay, 'tis true, there was never anything so sudden but the fight of two rams, and Caesar's thrasonical brag of 'I came, saw, and overcame.' For your brother and my sister no sooner met but they looked; no sooner looked, but they loved; no sooner loved, but they sighed; no sooner sighed, but they asked one another the reason; no sooner knew the reason, but they sought the remedy; and in these degrees have they made a pair of stairs to marriage, which they will climb incontinent – or else be incontinent before marriage. They are in the very wrath of love, and they will together – clubs cannot part them.

Orlando says that Oliver's joy at marriage will match his own sadness in not having Rosalind. She claims special powers, and promises he will marry her tomorrow. Phebe complains about Rosalind's unkind action.

1 'How bitter a thing it is …'

Orlando feels that his brother's happiness will be equalled by his own sorrow. His lines 34–5 have become a well-known saying. Give some examples from your own experience (or from your reading or viewing) that confirm or deny the truth of Orlando's saying.

2 A change of language?

Many people claim that Rosalind's manner and language changes from line 40, becoming more serious and formal, businesslike or ritualistic. Rosalind wants Orlando to believe she has benign magical powers and will ensure he marries Rosalind tomorrow, when Celia and Oliver marry.

How do you think Rosalind should deliver the lines: seriously, humorously, as a kind of ritual, or …? Experiment with different styles. Don't worry if you find the third sentence difficult to understand: most people do. It means something like: 'I say that you are intelligent, not to get you to think well of me; the only esteem I want is from helping you, not to improve my own reputation.'

3 Emphasis?

Would you advise Rosalind to emphasise 'him' in line 65? Why, or why not?

nuptial wedding
conceit understanding
grace me further my own reputation
damnable working with devils
gesture appearance
straits of fortune difficult circumstances
in sober meanings seriously
tender dearly hold precious
array clothes
despiteful scornful

ORLANDO They shall be married tomorrow and I will bid the duke to the nuptial. But O, how bitter a thing it is to look into happiness through another man's eyes. By so much the more shall I tomorrow be at the height of heart-heaviness, by how much I shall think my brother happy in having what he wishes for.

ROSALIND Why then, tomorrow, I cannot serve your turn for Rosalind?

ORLANDO I can live no longer by thinking.

ROSALIND I will weary you then no longer with idle talking. Know of me, then – for now I speak to some purpose – that I know you are a gentleman of good conceit. I speak not this that you should bear a good opinion of my knowledge, insomuch, I say, I know you are; neither do I labour for a greater esteem than may in some little measure draw a belief from you to do yourself good, and not to grace me. Believe then, if you please, that I can do strange things. I have, since I was three year old, conversed with a magician, most profound in his art, and yet not damnable. If you do love Rosalind so near the heart as your gesture cries it out, when your brother marries Aliena shall you marry her. I know into what straits of fortune she is driven, and it is not impossible to me, if it appear not inconvenient to you, to set her before your eyes tomorrow, human as she is, and without any danger.

ORLANDO Speak'st thou in sober meanings?

ROSALIND By my life, I do, which I tender dearly, though I say I am a magician. Therefore put you in your best array, bid your friends. For if you will be married tomorrow, you shall, and to Rosalind, if you will.

Enter SILVIUS *and* PHEBE

Look, here comes a lover of mine and a lover of hers.

PHEBE Youth, you have done me much ungentleness
To show the letter that I writ to you.

ROSALIND I care not if I have. It is my study
To seem despiteful and ungentle to you.
You are there followed by a faithful shepherd;
Look upon him, love him: he worships you.

As Silvius speaks his litany of what it is to love, Phebe, Orlando and Rosalind echo and endorse his feelings. Rosalind gives orders for them all to meet tomorrow, when their desires will be fulfilled.

Orlando, Rosalind, Silvius and Phebe. Work out how to stage all the script on the opposite page. Think about whether to use a comic or serious style of delivery, and the effect on the audience you wish to achieve.

fantasy imagination
observance respect
all trial enduring any hardship
Irish wolves (perhaps because of the monotony of their howling?)

PHEBE Good shepherd, tell this youth what 'tis to love.
SILVIUS It is to be all made of sighs and tears,
And so am I for Phebe.
PHEBE And I for Ganymede.
ORLANDO And I for Rosalind.
ROSALIND And I for no woman.
SILVIUS It is to be all made of faith and service,
And so am I for Phebe.
PHEBE And I for Ganymede.
ORLANDO And I for Rosalind.
ROSALIND And I for no woman.
SILVIUS It is to be all made of fantasy,
All made of passion, and all made of wishes,
All adoration, duty, and observance,
All humbleness, all patience, and impatience,
All purity, all trial, all obedience;
And so am I for Phebe.
PHEBE And so am I for Ganymede.
ORLANDO And so am I for Rosalind.
ROSALIND And so am I for no woman.
PHEBE [*To Rosalind*] If this be so, why blame you me to love you?
SILVIUS [*To Phebe*] If this be so, why blame you me to love you?
ORLANDO If this be so, why blame you me to love you?
ROSALIND Who do you speak to, 'Why blame you me to love you'?
ORLANDO To her that is not here, nor doth not hear.

ROSALIND Pray you no more of this, 'tis like the howling of Irish wolves against the moon. [*To Silvius*] I will help you, if I can. [*To Phebe*] I would love you, if I could. – Tomorrow meet me all together. – [*To Phebe*] I will marry you, if ever I marry woman, and I'll be married tomorrow. [*To Orlando*] I will satisfy you, if ever I satisfy man, and you shall be married tomorrow. [*To Silvius*] I will content you, if what pleases you contents you, and you shall be married tomorrow. [*To Orlando*] As you love Rosalind, meet; [*To Silvius*] As you love Phebe, meet – and as I love no woman, I'll meet. So, fare you well: I have left you commands.

SILVIUS I'll not fail, if I live.
PHEBE Nor I.
ORLANDO Nor I.

Exeunt

Touchstone and Audrey look forward to their marriage. The two pages sing of springtime as the time for young lovers, even though life is brief.

---

1 Sing it! (in pairs)

The pages' song seems to have two dramatic purposes. First, to mark the passage of time between Scenes 2 and 4 (between Rosalind's instructions to prepare for marriage and the ceremony in the final scene). Second, to echo the theme of love, now that all four lovers are preparing for marriage.

Step into role as the two pages and sing the song. The setting of a version of the song below was composed in 1600 by Thomas Morley. It is often used in theatre productions of the play, but feel free to make up your own tune.

---

woman of the world married woman

troth faith

clap into't roundly start immediately

hawking throat-clearing

prologues introductions

like two gipsies on a horse in unison

ring-time time for ringing wedding bells, giving marriage rings, dancing in rings

carol joyful song

Act 5 Scene 3
The Forest of Arden

Enter TOUCHSTONE and AUDREY

TOUCHSTONE Tomorrow is the joyful day, Audrey; tomorrow will we be married.

AUDREY I do desire it with all my heart, and I hope it is no dishonest desire to desire to be a woman of the world.

Enter two PAGES

Here come two of the banished duke's pages.

FIRST PAGE Well met, honest gentleman.

TOUCHSTONE By my troth, well met. Come, sit, sit, and a song.

SECOND PAGE We are for you; sit i'th'middle.

FIRST PAGE Shall we clap into't roundly, without hawking or spitting, or saying we are hoarse, which are the only prologues to a bad voice?

SECOND PAGE I'faith, i'faith, and both in a tune, like two gipsies on a horse.

FIRST AND SECOND PAGE It was a lover and his lass,
With a hey, and a ho, and a hey nonny-no,
That o'er the green cornfield did pass,
In spring-time,
The only pretty ring-time,
When birds do sing;
Hey ding a-ding, ding,
Sweet lovers love the spring.
Between the acres of the rye,
With a hey, and a ho, and a hey nonny-no,
These pretty country folks would lie,
In spring-time,
The only pretty ring-time,
When birds do sing;
Hey ding a-ding, ding,
Sweet lovers love the spring.
This carol they began that hour,
With a hey, and a ho, and a hey nonny-no,
How that a life was but a flower;
In spring-time,
The only pretty ring-time,

The pages sing of enjoying the present moment. Touchstone is unimpressed by their singing. Orlando is unsure if Ganymede can deliver his promises. Rosalind makes the duke and Orlando confirm their agreements.

---

1 *Carpe diem* – seize the day

The pages' song highlights the briefness of human life ('life was but a flower'). It urges that present happiness should be seized and enjoyed ('take the present time') when the season of springtime is perfect for lovers ('the prime'). The theme of the song is *carpe diem*, a Latin quotation meaning 'seize the day', taken from the Roman poet Horace (68–5BC).

Carpe diem has been a topic of literature and drama for over two thousand years. It is still much used today in all forms of culture. For example, it is the theme of the film *Dead Poets' Society*; and much popular music urges listeners to 'gather ye rosebuds while ye may'.

But Touchstone thinks it a waste of time to listen to 'such a foolish song'. His reaction to music seems rather like that of Jaques. Why do you think Shakespeare makes Touchstone ridicule the song? Step into role as Shakespeare and say why you include the song and have Touchstone mock it.

2 Promise-keeping

The final scene of the play begins in doubt, with Orlando uncertain whether Ganymede (Rosalind) can fulfil the promises he made. Turn the page for an activity on how Rosalind asks each character to keep their promises.

---

prime springtime, moment of perfection
ditty words of the song
untunable harsh, discordant
fear they hope fear their hope will not be fulfilled
whiles our compact is urged whilst our agreements are confirmed
bestow her on give her in marriage to

When birds do sing;
  Hey ding a-ding, ding,
Sweet lovers love the spring.
And therefore take the present time;
With a hey, and a ho, and a hey nonny-no,
For love is crownèd with the prime,
  In spring-time,
  The only pretty ring-time,
    When birds do sing;
  Hey ding a-ding, ding,
    Sweet lovers love the spring.

TOUCHSTONE Truly, young gentlemen, though there was no great matter in the ditty, yet the note was very untunable.

FIRST PAGE You are deceived, sir: we kept time; we lost not our time.

TOUCHSTONE By my troth, yes. I count it but time lost to hear such a foolish song. God buy you, and God mend your voices. – Come, Audrey.

Exeunt

Act 5 Scene 4
Duke Senior's camp in the forest

Enter DUKE SENIOR, AMIENS, JAQUES, ORLANDO, OLIVER, CELIA [as ALIENA]

DUKE SENIOR Dost thou believe, Orlando, that the boy
Can do all this that he hath promisèd?

ORLANDO I sometimes do believe and sometimes do not,
As those that fear they hope and know they fear.

Enter ROSALIND [*as* GANYMEDE], SILVIUS, *and* PHEBE

ROSALIND Patience once more whiles our compact is urged. –
You say, if I bring in your Rosalind,
You will bestow her on Orlando here?

DUKE SENIOR That would I, had I kingdoms to give with her.

ROSALIND And you say you will have her, when I bring her?

ORLANDO That would I, were I of all kingdoms king.

Rosalind promises to fulfil every character's wishes. Duke Senior and Orlando remark on Ganymede's resemblance to Rosalind. Touchstone boasts of his skills as a courtier.

1 Promise-keeping (in pairs)

In lines 5–25, Rosalind asks for patience while she gets each character to confirm their own promise: that Duke Senior will give his daughter in marriage to Orlando, that Orlando will marry her, and so on. Suggest a suitable style for Rosalind as she asks each character if they will do what they have agreed. Might she deliver her final lines 18–25 as a kind of magical spell or incantation?

2 Reminders of Rosalind

The exchange between Orlando and Duke Senior seems to confirm that Rosalind's disguise as Ganymede is still intact. But is it possible that Orlando has guessed the truth, yet wishes to keep the secret from her father? Advise Orlando how to speak lines 28–34. Should he heighten the 'magical' atmosphere of his final two lines?

3 From verse to prose

With the entry of Touchstone and Audrey, verse gives way to prose, the stage language for comedy (see page 178). Jaques' words recall the story of Noah's flood in the Bible. God warned Noah that the earth was to be flooded and that he should build an ark and fill it with pairs of every creature, however strange.

Touchstone lists the skills that prove he has been a courtier: dancing (a 'measure' is a stately dance), flattery, diplomacy and deceit ('politic'), false friendship ('smooth'), non-payment of bills (he has ruined – 'undone' – three tailors). You will find his skill as a quarreller on page 150.

---

all this matter even straighten everything out
lively touches lifelike marks
favour features, appearance
rudiments elements, first principles
desperate studies dangerous practices
Obscurèd hidden
motley-minded crazy-brained (see page 56)
purgation proof, test
ta'en up settled, reconciled, ended

ROSALIND You say you'll marry me, if I be willing.
PHEBE That will I, should I die the hour after.
ROSALIND But if you do refuse to marry me,
You'll give yourself to this most faithful shepherd.
PHEBE So is the bargain.
ROSALIND You say that you'll have Phebe if she will.
SILVIUS Though to have her and death were both one thing.
ROSALIND I have promised to make all this matter even. –
Keep you your word, O duke, to give your daughter. –
You yours, Orlando, to receive his daughter. –
Keep you your word, Phebe, that you'll marry me
Or else, refusing me, to wed this shepherd. –
Keep your word, Silvius, that you'll marry her
If she refuse me – and from hence I go
To make these doubts all even

Exeunt Rosalind and Celia

DUKE SENIOR I do remember in this shepherd boy
Some lively touches of my daughter's favour.
ORLANDO My lord, the first time that I ever saw him,
Methought he was a brother to your daughter;
But, my good lord, this boy is forest-born
And hath been tutored in the rudiments
Of many desperate studies by his uncle
Whom he reports to be a great magician,
Obscurèd in the circle of this forest.

Enter TOUCHSTONE *and* AUDREY

JAQUES There is sure another flood toward, and these couples are coming to the ark. Here comes a pair of very strange beasts which, in all tongues, are called fools.

TOUCHSTONE Salutation and greeting to you all.

JAQUES Good my lord, bid him welcome. This is the motley-minded gentleman that I have so often met in the forest: he hath been a courtier, he swears.

TOUCHSTONE If any man doubt that, let him put me to my purgation. I have trod a measure; I have flattered a lady; I have been politic with my friend, smooth with mine enemy; I have undone three tailors; I have had four quarrels, and like to have fought one.

JAQUES And how was that ta'en up?

TOUCHSTONE Faith, we met and found the quarrel was upon the seventh cause.

Touchstone declares that he too wishes to be married, because Audrey's ugliness conceals inner virtues. He lists the sequence of insults that lead up to a duel, and explains how to avoid the duel with an 'if'.

1 'An ill-favoured thing, sir, but mine own'

Touchstone's comparisons of Audrey with the wealthy miser in a poor house and the pearl in an oyster (lines 55–6) echoes the theme of appearance and reality. Audrey may not be outwardly attractive, but she has inner qualities. Suggest what Audrey is doing when Touchstone orders her 'Bear your body more seeming, Audrey' ('seeming' = decently).

2 The seventh cause: the etiquette of quarrelling

Touchstone lists how a quarrel develops, and how a fight can be avoided by an 'if'. Shakespeare is satirising the manuals on correct behaviour for courtiers which were written during the Elizabethan age. Many of these handbooks were about how to behave in a duel when one's honour had been insulted.

Explore ways of speaking and acting Touchstone's lines to bring out the humour. The table below shows the stages of a quarrel when an insult is repeated (another activity on the list is on page 159).

Name of response	Reply meaning	Result
1 Retort courteous	O yes it is	Avoid duel
2 Quip modest	It's my affair	Ditto
3 Reply churlish	You are a poor judge	Ditto
4 Reproof valiant	That isn't true	Ditto
5 Countercheck quarrelsome	You lie	Ditto
6 Lie circumstantial	You lie, because ...	Ditto
7 Lie direct	You definitely lie	Duel!

God'ild ... like God reward you and all of you
copulatives lovers
swift and sententious quick-witted and full of wise sayings
bolt arrow
dulcet diseases sweet weaknesses
circumstantial circumlocutionary (beating about the bush)
durst dared
measured swords checked our swords were of equal length
take up settle
swore brothers promised friendship

JAQUES How, 'seventh cause'? – Good my lord, like this fellow.

DUKE SENIOR I like him very well.

TOUCHSTONE God'ild you, sir; I desire you of the like. I press in here, sir, amongst the rest of the country copulatives, to swear and to forswear according as marriage binds and blood breaks. A poor virgin, sir, an ill-favoured thing, sir, but mine own. A poor humour of mine, sir, to take that that no man else will. Rich honesty dwells like a miser, sir, in a poor house, as your pearl in your foul oyster.

DUKE SENIOR By my faith, he is very swift and sententious.

TOUCHSTONE According to 'the fool's bolt', sir, and such dulcet diseases.

JAQUES But, for 'the seventh cause': how did you find the quarrel on 'the seventh cause'?

TOUCHSTONE Upon a lie seven times removed. – Bear your body more seeming, Audrey. – As thus, sir: I did dislike the cut of a certain courtier's beard. He sent me word, if I said his beard was not cut well, he was in the mind it was: this is called 'the retort courteous'. If I sent him word again it was not well cut, he would send me word he cut it to please himself: this is called 'the quip modest'. If again it was not well cut, he disabled my judgement: this is called 'the reply churlish'. If again it was not well cut, he would answer I spake not true: this is called 'the reproof valiant'. If again it was not well cut, he would say I lied: this is called 'the countercheck quarrelsome'. And so to 'the lie circumstantial' and 'the lie direct'.

JAQUES And how oft did you say his beard was not well cut?

TOUCHSTONE I durst go no further than the lie circumstantial, nor he durst not give me the lie direct; and so we measured swords, and parted.

JAQUES Can you nominate, in order now, the degrees of the lie?

TOUCHSTONE O sir, we quarrel in print, by the book – as you have books for good manners. I will name you the degrees: the first, the retort courteous; the second, the quip modest; the third, the reply churlish; the fourth, the reproof valiant; the fifth, the countercheck quarrelsome; the sixth, the lie with circumstance; the seventh, the lie direct. All these you may avoid but the lie direct, and you may avoid that too with an 'if'. I knew when seven justices could not take up a quarrel but when the parties were met themselves, one of them thought but of an 'if': as, 'If you said so, then I said so.' And they shook hands and swore brothers. Your 'if' is the only peacemaker: much virtue in 'if'.

Duke Senior praises Touchstone. Hymen enters with Rosalind and Celia (undisguised) and asks the duke to receive his daughter. Rosalind promises to be Orlando's wife. Hymen ordains four marriages.

1 Praising Touchstone

The duke says that Touchstone uses the disguise of foolishness to ensure his witty comments find their mark (a 'stalking-horse' is a real or imitation horse behind which a hunter hides to shoot his prey). How might Touchstone acknowledge the duke's praise?

2 Enter Hymen (in groups of any size)

The entry of Hymen, the Greek and Roman god of marriage, is a great moment of theatre. Work out a staging of lines 93–134 using the following to help you:

a The episode may have been staged as a masque. Masques were spectacular entertainments which drew imaginatively on classical mythology to present gods and goddesses. They used elaborate scenery and costumes, and were filled with music, poetry and dance. Masques revelled in visual effects, often using complex stage machinery and lighting to create striking illusions.

b Will you present Hymen as a god, or as a character (for example, Adam)?

c Hymen's language is formal and ritualistic and uses rhyming verse. Will you emphasise the rhymes?

d 'If truth holds true contents.' Line 114 puzzles everyone. One critic has suggested it has at least 168 possible interpretations! Two are 'If revealing who Ganymede and Aliena really are brings genuine happiness', or 'If the couples remain true to their vows'. Make one or two suggestions of your own.

Still music solemn and quiet music
Atone together are reconciled
bar confusion forbid misunderstandings
Hymen's bands marriage vows
cross troubles, quarrels
accord consent
sure together bound fast
That reason, wonder may diminish explanation will reduce your amazement

JAQUES Is not this a rare fellow, my lord? He's as good at anything, and yet a fool.

DUKE SENIOR He uses his folly like a stalking-horse, and under the presentation of that he shoots his wit.

Still music. Enter HYMEN, [*with*] ROSALIND, *and* CELIA [*as themselves*]

HYMEN Then is there mirth in heaven,
When earthly things made even
Atone together.
Good duke, receive thy daughter;
Hymen from heaven brought her,
Yea, brought her hither
That thou mightst join her hand with his,
Whose heart within his bosom is.

ROSALIND [*To the Duke*] To you I give myself, for I am yours.
[*To Orlando*] To you I give myself, for I am yours.

DUKE SENIOR If there be truth in sight, you are my daughter.

ORLANDO If there be truth in sight, you are my Rosalind.

PHEBE If sight and shape be true, why then, my love, adieu.

ROSALIND [*To the Duke*] I'll have no father, if you be not he.
[*To Orlando*] I'll have no husband, if you be not he.
[*To Phebe*] Nor ne'er wed woman, if you be not she.

HYMEN Peace, ho: I bar confusion,
'Tis I must make conclusion
Of these most strange events.
Here's eight that must take hands
To join in Hymen's bands,
If truth holds true contents.
[*To Orlando and Rosalind*] You and you no cross shall part.
[*To Oliver and Celia*] You and you are heart in heart.
[*To Phebe*] You to his love must accord,
Or have a woman to your lord.
[*To Touchstone and Audrey*] You and you are sure together
As the winter to foul weather. –
Whiles a wedlock hymn we sing,
Feed yourselves with questioning,
That reason, wonder may diminish
How thus we met and these things finish.

After the song celebrating marriage and fertility, Phebe accepts Silvius. Jaques de Boys brings news of Duke Frederick's conversion and penitence. Duke Senior orders revelry.

---

1 Staging decisions

All the following are matters that are decided in each new production of the play. Give reasons for your own solutions.

a Who might sing the song: Hymen? Amiens? everyone?

b How does Phebe accept Silvius at lines 133–4: grudgingly, willingly, or ...?

c How do Oliver and Orlando respond to the sight of their brother?

d The news of Duke Frederick's conversion is sudden and improbable. But its unlikely surprise is part of the pastoral romance tradition which Shakespeare was satirising in *As You Like It* (see pages 176–7). That tradition delighted in happy endings in which order was restored with reconciliations, conversions to goodness, forgiveness, marriages, and the prospect of harmony for individuals and society. How would you wish the audience to respond to the news of Frederick's conversion?

e Does the duke acknowledge Orlando, through his marriage to Rosalind, as the heir to the dukedom? ('potent' in line 153 can mean 'powerful' or 'potential').

f How does Jaques de Boys deliver his news? Does he make many pauses (for example, to add dramatic effect to his report, or when he recognises his brothers)?

g For more on Duke Frederick's meeting with the 'old religious man', see page 159, activity **10**.

Juno goddess of marriage
board and bed family life
High wedlock blessed marriage
fancy love
resorted to took refuge in
Addressed a mighty power prepared a huge army
conduct leadership
offer'st fairly bring a fine gift
shrewd sharp, harsh
the measure of their states their social status
new-fall'n dignity newly acquired honour (his dukedom)

Song Wedding is great Juno's crown,
O blessed bond of board and bed.
'Tis Hymen peoples every town,
High wedlock then be honourèd.
Honour, high honour, and renown
To Hymen, god of every town.

DUKE SENIOR O my dear niece: welcome thou art to me,
Even daughter; welcome in no less degree.

PHEBE I will not eat my word now thou art mine:
Thy faith my fancy to thee doth combine.

Enter [JAQUES DE BOYS, *the*] *second brother*

JAQUES DE BOYS Let me have audience for a word or two.
I am the second son of old Sir Roland,
That bring these tidings to this fair assembly.
Duke Frederick, hearing how that every day
Men of great worth resorted to this forest,
Addressed a mighty power which were on foot
In his own conduct, purposely to take
His brother here and put him to the sword;
And to the skirts of this wild wood he came,
Where, meeting with an old religious man,
After some question with him, was converted
Both from his enterprise and from the world,
His crown bequeathing to his banished brother,
And all their lands restored to them again
That were with him exiled. This to be true,
I do engage my life.

DUKE SENIOR Welcome, young man.
Thou offer'st fairly to thy brothers' wedding:
To one his lands withheld, and to the other
A land itself at large, a potent dukedom. –
First, in this forest, let us do those ends
That here were well begun and well begot;
And after every of this happy number
That have endured shrewd days and nights with us
Shall share the good of our returnèd fortune
According to the measure of their states.
Meantime forget this new-fall'n dignity
And fall into our rustic revelry. –

Jaques resolves to join Duke Frederick. He predicts honour and success to all except Touchstone, and declines to join the celebrations. Rosalind asks the audience to approve the play with their applause.

---

1 'True delights'? (in groups of any size)

The duke orders 'With measure heaped in joy to th'measures fall' (with overflowing joy, begin dancing). Work out how you would stage the final dance ('rites' = wedding ceremonies).

2 Jaques rejects the merry-making

Jaques refuses to join in the celebrations, preferring to join Duke Frederick in abandoning court life ('convertites' = religious converts). Why do you think Shakespeare adds this 'serious' episode into the closing festivities?

3 Breaking the illusion?

Should Rosalind stay in role as she speaks the Epilogue, or should she address the audience as an actor, rather than as the character? Experiment with both styles of delivering the Epilogue, adding stage business (for example, in one production, Rosalind removed her wedding dress to reveal she was wearing a modern sweater and jeans).

4 'If I were a woman'

Line 13 is a reminder that in Shakespeare's time all actors were male, and Rosalind was probably played by a boy or very young man. But today nearly all Rosalinds are female. Decide whether you would rewrite the line for a female actor.

5 Final image (in pairs)

Suggest the final 'stage picture' the audience will see in your production of the play. Give your reasons for that final image.

---

thrown into neglect rejected
Is but … victualled has supplies for only two months
pastime fun and games
bush advertisement (wine merchants hung an ivy branch outside their shops)
insinuate with slyly persuade
furnished dressed
become me be appropriate
conjure charm, enchant
simpering silly smiling
defied disliked

Play, music – and you, brides and bridegrooms all,
With measure heaped in joy to th'measures fall.

JAQUES Sir, by your patience. [*To Jaques de Boys*] If I heard you rightly,
The duke hath put on a religious life
And thrown into neglect the pompous court.

JAQUES DE BOYS He hath.

JAQUES To him will I: out of these convertites
There is much matter to be heard and learned.
[*To the Duke*] You to your former honour I bequeath:
Your patience and your virtue well deserves it.
[*To Orlando*] You to a love that your true faith doth merit.
[*To Oliver*] You to your land and love and great allies.
[*To Silvius*] You to a long and well-deservèd bed.
[*To Touchstone*] And you to wrangling, for thy loving voyage
Is but for two months victualled. – So to your pleasures,
I am for other than for dancing measures.

DUKE SENIOR Stay, Jaques, stay.

JAQUES To see no pastime, I. What you would have
I'll stay to know at your abandoned cave. *Exit*

DUKE SENIOR Proceed, proceed. – We will begin these rites
As we do trust they'll end, in true delights.

[*They dance.*] *Exeunt all but Rosalind who speaks the Epilogue:*

ROSALIND It is not the fashion to see the lady the Epilogue, but it is no more unhandsome than to see the lord the Prologue. If it be true that good wine needs no bush, 'tis true that a good play needs no Epilogue. Yet to good wine they do use good bushes, and good plays prove the better by the help of good Epilogues. What a case am I in, then, that am neither a good Epilogue nor cannot insinuate with you in the behalf of a good play? I am not furnished like a beggar, therefore to beg will not become me. My way is to conjure you, and I'll begin with the women. I charge you, O women, for the love you bear to men, to like as much of this play as please you. – And I charge you, O men, for the love you bear to women – as I perceive by your simpering none of you hates them – that between you and the women the play may please. If I were a woman, I would kiss as many of you as had beards that pleased me, complexions that liked me, and breaths that I defied not. And I am sure as many as have good beards, or good faces, or sweet breaths will, for my kind offer, when I make curtsey, bid me farewell. *Exit*

Looking back at the play

Activities for groups or individuals

1 End with a song?

Some productions of *As You Like It* end with the whole company on stage singing a song from the play. Which song would you choose for everyone to sing at the final curtain? Give reasons for your choice.

2 Alternative title

Invent an alternative title for the play, for example, *The Triumph of Love*, or *Brides and Bridegrooms All*, or *True Delights*, and so on.

3 Duke Frederick reports

In one production of the play, Duke Frederick himself, rather than Jaques de Boys, entered as messenger to report his conversion. Turn to Act 5 Scene 4, lines 135–50 and rewrite the speech as it might be delivered by Duke Frederick.

4 Did Shakespeare believe it?

Did Shakespeare believe in the Forest of Arden as a rural idyll where happiness and community spirit reigned? Or was his intention to subvert the notion of that ideal world, showing its impossibility? Hotseat Shakespeare about his intentions in writing *As You Like It*.

5 Reconcilement, merriment ...?

Brainstorm a list of words to describe the atmosphere you would wish to create at the end of a stage production of *As You Like It*. Suggest how you would play the final episode from the entry of Hymen to create the mood you feel most appropriate.

6 Happy ever after?

Jaques says that Touchstone and Audrey's happiness will not last, and they will soon fall to quarrelling. Is he right? Step into role as Touchstone and write your autobiography for the five-year period after the end of the play.

7 The exiled lord's story

You are one of the lords who followed Duke Senior into exile in the Forest of Arden. Tell your story. Include your reasons for your flight from court, life in the forest and your return to court.

8 Holiday brochure or holiday programme

The Forest of Arden only exists in the imagination (see pages 172–3). But what if it really were an actual place? Become the Tourism Officer for the Forest of Arden. Prepare your publicity brochure designed to attract people to spend their holidays there. Or become a television presenter for a holiday programme. Present your travelogue.

9 A modern *Rule Book for Quarrellers*

In Act 5 Scene 4, Touchstone says 'we quarrel in print, by the book' (line 78), and tells how cowardly courtiers use language to avoid having to fight. He lists the seven stages of a quarrel, and shows that after all the formal exchanges of insults, actual violence can be avoided with an 'if'!

What would a modern *Rule Book for Quarrellers* look like? Use the table on page 150 to help you make up a contemporary version of seven rules of how to avoid a quarrel.

10 A missing scene?

Dr Samuel Johnson, the famous Shakespeare editor and critic, thought that Shakespeare missed an opportunity to teach a moral lesson in not writing a scene showing Duke Frederick's meeting with the 'old religious man'. Remind youself of the report of the meeting (Act 5 Scene 4, lines 138–49). Then try your hand at writing this 'missing scene'. It shows what happened to Duke Frederick that explains his conversion and penitence, and his decision to withdraw from the world, and to restore all his ill-gotten land and titles back to their rightful owners.

11 Girl power

'This play is all about girl power', said one student. In what ways is that claim true and untrue?

What is *As You Like It* about?

Story

Before the play begins, Duke Frederick has overthrown his brother, Duke Senior, the rightful ruler, who now lives in exile in the Forest of Arden. The play opens with a clash between another pair of brothers, the sons of Sir Roland de Boys: Orlando is mistreated by his elder brother, Oliver, who plans to kill him.

At a wrestling match, Rosalind, the daughter of Duke Senior, falls in love with Orlando and he with her. Orlando defeats the wrestler Charles, but is dismissed as an enemy by Duke Frederick, who also banishes Rosalind on pain of death. Disguised as a boy, Ganymede, Rosalind flees to the Forest of Arden with Celia, Duke Frederick's daughter. They take Touchstone, the court jester, with them. Orlando also flees to Arden to escape his brother's murderous intentions.

In the forest, Rosalind and Celia buy a sheep farm, intending to live as country folk. They meet Orlando who has hung love poems to Rosalind on the trees. The disguised Rosalind promises to cure him of his love. He thinks she is a boy and obeys her command to woo her as Rosalind. Meanwhile, Duke Senior enjoys forest life and is amused by a courtier, the melancholy Jaques, who sets himself up as a critic of all human folly and weakness.

The forest reveals different aspects of love. Touchstone plans to marry Audrey, a goatherd. Silvius, a shepherd, loves Phebe, a disdainful shepherdess. She rejects him, but she falls in love with the disguised Rosalind.

At the end of the play, all the complications seem resolved. Orlando saves the life of his brother Oliver, who becomes converted to goodness and falls in love with Celia. Rosalind abandons her disguise, causing Phebe to accept Silvius. Hymen, the Greek and Roman god of marriage, announces the weddings of Rosalind and Orlando, and the other three couples. Duke Frederick, also converted to goodness, restores the dukedom to Duke Senior, and everyone except Jaques plans to return to the court. Jaques prefers to join Duke Frederick and to reject the everyday world of happiness.

- Write your own story of the play in exactly 50 words.

Title

The title of the play may be Shakespeare's hint as to its meaning. *As You Like It* may be Shakespeare saying to his Elizabethan audiences, 'Here's a play like those other successful plays of mine you've enjoyed recently. This is the mixture as before, another fairy-tale. Like *A Midsummer Night's Dream* or *The Two Gentlemen of Verona*, this is going to be another comedy about the trials of love, girls dressing up as boys, forests – and a happy ending with multiple marriages! This is how you like it.'

Another way of thinking about the title is to see it as Shakespeare's assurance that the play will be as *you* like it. In other words, whoever you are, whatever your social background and interests, there's something here for you. All kinds of meanings and interpretations are possible. It can be enjoyed at all different levels. There's something in it for everyone. If you like spectacle, some violent action, songs, clowns and jokes, disguise, lots of talk about love, and the silliness that people in love get up to, then this is the play for you, this is to your taste.

The title may also promise Elizabethan audiences that they will find many reminders of their own world. In Jaques, they will see the malcontent, the world-weary cynic who was such a familiar figure in Shakespeare's London. They will recognise some of their contemporaries in Jaques' 'seven ages of man' speech: brave soldiers, justices who accepted bribes, and so on. When Phebe speaks of the 'dead shepherd' who wrote 'whoever loved that loved not at first sight?', some audience members would recall it had been written by the playwright Christopher Marlowe. He had been killed in a tavern brawl only a few years earlier.

The educated members of Shakespeare's audience would especially like the play for its many literary, biblical and classical allusions. They recognised in the play the influence of the books they read for pleasure, picking up its references to the Roman poet Ovid, and the various elements of Greek mythology. They enjoyed how Shakespeare presented one of the hot topics of the day among the educated elite: whether poetry was true and sincere, or simply pretence or 'feigning'. When they heard that argument put into the mouths of a clown and a goatherd, Touchstone and Audrey, those audience members saw the debate being given a novel twist by their favourite playwright.

- Invent your own title for the play. Explain why it is appropriate.

Court versus country – 'Under the greenwood tree'

The tradition of pastoral romance which so strongly influenced Shakespeare as he wrote *As You Like It* portrayed rural life as an ideal world of innocence and freedom. It was a world into which kings and queens and courtiers could escape. Disguised as shepherds and shepherdesses, they could enjoy the tranquillity and harmony of country life.

On the surface, Shakespeare seems to follow that tradition. The play is full of contrasts between court and country. The court is an unnatural and unhappy place; the country is natural and joyful. The court is corrupt and artificial, a world to escape from; the country is benign and delightful, a place of freedom.

Duke Senior declares the opposition between the two worlds in his first speech 'Are not these woods/More free from peril than the envious court?'. Touchstone and Corin debate their contrasting views of court and country life. Amiens sings of the pleasures of life under the greenwood tree where there is 'No enemy/But winter and rough weather'. Another of his songs tells of 'man's ingratitude' and of false friendship ('Most friendship is feigning') in contrast to life under the green holly. In the court, brother is set against brother, and ambition, envy and intrigue are common. Duke Frederick has usurped his brother, and he exiles Rosalind on pain of death. In contrast, the exiles in the Forest of Arden seem to live contentedly as a friendly community.

But Shakespeare's portrayal of the theme of town versus country is not a simple opposition of bad versus good. The Forest of Arden is not an idealised utopia. Its winds are biting, an 'icy fang'. The man who employs Corin is a hard taskmaster, Phebe cruelly scorns the besotted Silvius. The deer are hunted to death by the exiled lords, and snakes and lions threaten life. Duke Senior maintains the hierarchy of the court. Jaques cynically comments on the foolishness of the man who leaves 'his wealth and ease' for the rough pleasures of the forest. Audrey is quite unlike the idealised shepherdess of the romantic tradition.

At the end of the play, the exiles prepare to return to court. They do not seem unhappy to be leaving the country behind them. Only Jaques, the cynic, prefers to stay behind, and his purpose is not the enjoyment of the innocent pleasures of rural life.

- Devise a dramatic presentation that contrasts 'court' and 'country'.

Love – 'What think you of falling in love?'

Love is the driving force of the play. Within a few minutes of her first appearance, Rosalind asks the question 'what think you of falling in love?'. The rest of the play enables you to explore your responses to her question as it presents many different kinds of love.

- *Brotherly love*: Orlando saves Oliver from a lion.
- *Love as friendship and service*: the devotion of Adam to Orlando and his father (and Orlando's compassion towards him).
- *Self love*: Jaques' delight in his pose as cynic and world-weary traveller, promoting his image as malcontent.
- *Love as lust*: the sexual desire of Touchstone for Audrey.
- *Idealised love*: Silvius' doting worship of Phebe; Orlando's bad verses.
- *The cruelty of love*: Phebe's scorn for Silvius.
- *Sincere love*: Rosalind for Orlando, in all its changing moods.
- *Love at first sight*: Orlando and Rosalind, Celia and Oliver, Phebe for Rosalind.

Rosalind fully displays the range of emotions that lovers feel. She is downcast at Orlando's lateness. She fires a breathless list of questions at Celia, demanding to know who has written poems to her. She delights in hearing Celia talk about Orlando, and relishes the flirting and word play in the wooing scene. She expresses sheer exuberance in 'O coz, coz, coz …', and faints at the sight of a handkerchief stained with her lover's blood. But Rosalind's love is also clearsighted and sceptical. She is not fooled by the bad verses that Orlando writes, and she mocks his claim that he will love for ever and a day. There is stark realism in her recognition that 'men have died … but not for love'.

As You Like It explores a variety of viewpoints as characters express and criticise the absurdities and contradictions of love. But in spite of (or perhaps because of) all the trials and tribulations of love, the play ends happily in the marriages of the four pairs of lovers.

- Find a way of showing how love affects Rosalind at ten different moments in the play (for example, as a series of tableaux, or different moods).

Appearance and reality – 'Most friendship is feigning'

Things are not as they seem in *As You Like It*. Oliver deceives Charles about Orlando. Amiens sings of false friendship. Touchstone and Audrey talk together of feigning in poetry. The seemingly benign Forest of Arden conceals hardships and dangers. There is death for the deer, exhaustion for the newly arrived Celia, a hard master for Corin and threatening snakes and lions. The play sets a continuing puzzle about the nature of the different types of love it portrays: which are real and which are merely pretence?

The most obvious way in which the play explores the theme of appearance and reality is through disguise. Celia, a princess, disguises herself as Aliena, a shepherdess. Rosalind disguises herself as a youth, the boy Ganymede, and fools the inhabitants of the forest. Most notably she uses her disguise to trick Orlando into wooing her. But her disguise also causes Phebe to fall in love with her, deceived by her appearance.

Some characters are aware that things are not as they seem, others are duped by outward show. Celia always knows that Ganymede is Rosalind in disguise, but Orlando does not. He thinks she is a boy. Under cover of her disguise, Rosalind can speak as she really feels, and enjoy Orlando's wooing. The deception heightens dramatic irony (when the audience knows more than a character on stage). Orlando does not recognise the truth of what Rosalind says, but the audience does.

Shakespeare's own audience would be intrigued by the multiple layering of appearance and reality. In his time, women were forbidden to act, so all parts were played by males. In 1599, an audience would have seen a boy, playing a girl, playing a boy, playing a girl asking to be wooed. This may sound absurd, but audiences over the ages have willingly suspended disbelief and enjoyed the ambiguities that arise from cross-dressing.

- Turn to four pages at random. What evidence of false appearance can you find on each?

Order and disorder – 'There begins my sadness'

Many Shakespeare plays begin with a portrait of an ordered world which is rapidly thrown into disorder by some violent action. But in *As You Like It*, Shakespeare's treatment of the theme of order and disorder is somewhat different from other plays. The play begins with a portrait of disorder. Orlando is in rebellion about his cruel treatment by his brother. Duke Frederick has already overthrown his brother and seized his dukedom.

So before the play begins, the social and moral fabric has been disrupted. The long middle section takes place in the peaceful world of Arden. Such disorder as exists is shown as the trials of love. The play ends with order restored. Orlando and Oliver are reconciled, four marriages are proclaimed, and Duke Senior is returned to his rightful position of duke.

- Some stage productions portray the theme of order and disorder by staging the Forest of Arden as a harsh, winter setting which changes to one of high summer for the celebrations of marriage and happiness at the end of the play. How would you express the theme in a production?

Time – 'There's no clock in the forest'

After the hectic speed of the first Act, time seems to stand still in the Forest of Arden. There, time is discussed in various ways. Rosalind claims that 'Time travels at different speeds', and gives examples of its 'divers paces'. Touchstone remarks mordantly on time: 'and so from hour to hour we rot and rot'. Jaques' 'seven ages of man' is the play's best-known expression of the passage of time. The forest itself marks a time of holiday. But holidays don't last forever, and at the end the duke and his court leave Arden.

- Draw a large clock face. Plot the progress of the play on it.

Change

As with every Shakespeare play, 'change' is a major theme of *As You Like It.* Celia and Rosalind disguise themselves as Aliena and Ganymede, changing from princesses to a shepherdess and her brother. At the end of the play, both return to their status as princesses. Orlando begins penniless, a victim of his brother's hatred. He ends married to Duke Senior's daughter, and with the prospect of becoming heir to the dukedom. The 'villains' of Act 1, Oliver and Duke Frederick, are converted to goodness in the final scenes. But Jaques seems unchanged at the play's end.

- Consider each character in turn. Describe how they change, if at all, over the course of the play (in social status; moral awareness or understanding; learning about others, or love, or themselves).

Characters

Rosalind

Rosalind is one of the longest parts in all Shakespeare. She has more lines than Macbeth or Prospero. Rosalind appears first as a typical court lady, enjoying witty wordplay with her cousin Celia. In her early scenes, she seems to accept a subordinate role to Celia (it is Celia's suggestion that they leave the court and go to Arden). But as the play moves to the forest, and in her disguise as Ganymede, Rosalind takes the initiative more and more. She controls the action, manipulating other characters and exercising her strong sense of humour as she alternately mocks and celebrates love.

As Rosalind's behaviour changes, so too does her language. She abandons the flowery style of the court in favour of direct and frank analyses of love. She gives full expression to her feelings: 'O coz, coz, coz, my pretty little coz, that thou didst know how many fathom deep I am in love!'

In the forest, disguised as Ganymede, Rosalind woos and tests Orlando, with whom she is head over heels in love. Even in her disguise she retains her feminity, keeping Orlando at a distance as he suggests a kiss: 'Nay, you were better speak first'. She uses her disguise to conceal and to reveal her true feelings: 'Come, woo me, woo me; for now I am in a holiday humour and like enough to consent'. And consent she does, tricking Orlando into marrying her, putting the words of the wedding ceremony into his mouth ('I take thee, Rosalind, for wife'), and joyously replying 'I do take thee, Orlando, for my husband'.

Rosalind's mood swings violently as she experiences the conflicting emotions of love. But for all her rapture, she is clear-eyed about the nature of love: 'men have died from time to time – and worms have eaten them – but not for love'. That sceptical attitude does not prevent her feelings getting the better of her: she faints at the sight of Orlando's blood-stained napkin. Rosalind finally becomes a kind of mistress of ceremonies, arranging the happy ending of multiple marriages. In the Epilogue, Shakespeare adds yet another layer to Rosalind's changeability when his boy actor acknowledges the cross-dressing role: 'If I were a woman'.

In the court and in the country. Rosalind changes from Elizabethan court lady to the youth Ganymede in traditional doublet and hose. Compare these pictures with other images of Rosalind on pages 33, 109, 114, 142 and 172, then create your own designs for her costumes.

Orlando – 'Gentle, strong, and valiant'

Like Rosalind, Orlando is wrongly treated by a close relative who hates him only for his goodness. His eldest brother denies him education and money, and plans to murder him. After defeating Charles the wrestler, Orlando flees to the Forest of Arden with Adam, his old servant. In the forest, he takes on the role of a foolish courtly lover, writing bad verses to his beloved Rosalind and hanging them on trees. But Rosalind, in disguise as Ganymede, persuades him to woo her, and he discovers true love. Towards the end of the play he is wounded as he saves his wicked brother Oliver from a hungry lion. At the end of the play, he is about to marry Rosalind and is heir to Duke Senior.

Oliver – 'The enemy of all your graces'

Oliver ignores his father's dying wishes. He refuses to give Orlando the wealth, status and schooling that is properly due to him. Early in the play, Oliver appears violent and ruthless. But he is converted to goodness by Orlando's selfless action in saving him from death in the forest. He falls instantly in love with Celia, gives all his lands and possessions to Orlando and looks forward to marriage.

Duke Frederick – 'With his eyes full of anger'

Duke Frederick is the usurper who has seized his brother's dukedom. Injustice and vindictiveness reign in his court. He threatens Rosalind with death, maltreats Oliver and leads an army to Arden to kill his brother. But he meets an old religious man, is converted, gives up all his wickedness and resolves to live the life of a simple hermit.

Duke Senior – 'Sweet are the uses of adversity'

Duke Senior has been deposed by his brother. In the Forest of Arden, he relishes the lessons that country life can teach. He gladly gives hospitality to Orlando and Adam. At the end of the play, he is happy to return to court life.

Corin – 'I am a true labourer'

Corin is content in his modest life as a shepherd in the forest. He has served a hard master, but finds better employment with Celia and Rosalind. He counsels Silvius about love and endures Touchstone's condescension with good humour.

Touchstone – 'The motley-minded gentleman'

Touchstone is the jester who joins Rosalind and Celia in their flight to the Forest of Arden. His role in court was that of licensed fool: to comment on what he saw around him, exposing folly and dishonesty. His name signifies his dramatic function. A touchstone was used to find if a metal was true gold. Touchstone similarly tests the genuineness of characters with his sceptical comments. But as Celia reminds him, he could be whipped for speaking the truth.

Touchstone, like Jaques, is a mocking observer. He shows up the sham honour and courtesy of the court, and he ridicules love, melancholy and the country. Touchstone loves language, delighting in stories, puns, jokes, sexual double entendres and false logic. His love for Audrey is quite different from the other types of love portrayed in the play.

In this all male production at London's National Theatre, Anthony Hopkins played Audrey, and Derek Jacobi was Touchstone.

Silvius and Phebe – 'tame snake' and 'proud disdain'

Elizabethans would recognise the pair as stock characters from pastoral literature. Speaking in elegant, polished verse, they are traditional figures of the court in the country (rather like Marie Antoinette, who, before the French Revolution, created an idealised rural idyll without dirt or labour where she and her attendants dressed up as shepherdesses and shepherds). Silvius is the lovelorn faithful shepherd who suffers the pains of unrequited love. Phebe is the disdainful shepherdess, the cruel mistress of pastoral literature, whose beautiful face conceals a hard heart. She rejects and humiliates Silvius, but falls for Rosalind disguised as Ganymede. When Rosalind throws off her disguise, Phebe agrees to marry Silvius.

Celia – 'Let my father seek another heir!'

Celia is daughter of the wicked Duke Frederick, and cousin and best friend of Rosalind. She stands up to her angry father, and proposes the plan of escape to Arden where she disguises herself as a shepherdess. She seems to become more reserved as the play progresses, taking a subordinate role to Rosalind and having less and less to say (she is silent in Act 5). As you think about Celia, ask yourself: Is she genuinely critical of Rosalind in the wooing episode? Does she become increasingly separated from Rosalind, aware that she is losing her best friend?

Adam – 'O good old man'

Adam represents an older world of loyal and faithful service. He gives his life savings to Orlando, and goes with him into exile in Arden. He disappears from the play after Act 2. What happens to him?

Audrey – 'Bear your body more seeming, Audrey'

Audrey is a goatherd, simple and down to earth. Unlike Phebe or Celia, she is a 'real' shepherdess. On stage, Audrey is often played as a dirty, rough country wench.

- Use the descriptions on pages 166–71 as the starting point for your investigation of a chosen character. Identify each scene in which your character appears, and suggest their motives for speaking and acting as they do, together with how you think other characters view them.

Jaques – 'They say you are a melancholy fellow'

Today, the melancholy Jaques would probably be called neurotic or unbalanced. He is the malcontent, a familiar role in Elizabethan times, a sardonic observer who comments cynically on everything and everybody around him, seeing only foolishness, absurdities and ingratitude. He has a jaundiced, pessimistic view of the world, and would almost certainly agree with Hamlet's description of it as 'weary, stale, flat and unprofitable'. Duke Senior accuses him of having been 'a libertine' who now wishes to make the world as corrupt as himself.

As you think about Jaques' character, explore possible answers to some of the following questions: Is he playing a role to hide his true feelings? Why does Duke Senior enjoy his company? Does he have a genuine sense of humour? What do you make of his final decision not to take part in the celebrations, but to join Duke Frederick in rejecting court life? Audrey calls him 'the old gentleman'. How old is he? What is your own attitude to Jaques?

Does his character show in his face?
Jaques at Shakespeare's Globe Theatre 1998.

The Forest of Arden

The Forest of Arden is a place of escape to the illusion of perpetual holiday and freedom. It is a place where time stands still ('There's no clock in the forest'). This contented never-never land of make-believe exists under many names: Utopia, the Big Rock Candy Mountain, fairyland, Xanadu, Arcadia, the Land of Cockaigne, the Golden Age, Shangri-La, Camelot, New Atlantis, Blue-remembered hills, Dreamland. It is the biblical Garden of Eden in the days before the Fall.

Shakespeare created similar remote worlds in other plays: Illyria in *Twelfth Night*, the wood near Athens in *A Midsummer Night's Dream*, Belmont in *The Merchant of Venice*, Ephesus in *The Comedy of Errors*. These are festive worlds of romance, full of magical possibilities, where anything can happen. In these exotic locations of Shakespeare's comedies, disguises are adopted, all kinds of confusions, errors and mistakes occur, but the end result is marriage and happiness. All are places where dreams come true.

The myth of the Forest of Arden sees it as a place of perpetual springtime or summer. It is an enchanted innocent world where happiness is truly possible, where community, brotherhood and welcoming hospitality are found. It fosters regeneration and reconciliation as characters are changed by their experience, discovering truths about themselves and others. As Charles, the wrestler, says, Arden is like the 'golden world' of Robin Hood and his Merry Men.

Arden is a refuge from the hypocrisy, deceit and ambition of the court. It is a place of harmony, free from the anger of fathers and brothers, from envy and malice, or the false friendship of flattering courtiers. In modern times, many attempts have been made to find similar places of escape and freedom from the realities of everyday life: hippy communes, organic communities, drop-outs.

But, as all the idealistic descriptions above suggest, the Forest of Arden is a fictitious place, a state of mind. It is not the countryside near Stratford-upon-Avon, or the Ardenne region of eastern France. Rather, it is a world which exists in the imagination for a few hours on stage as the play is performed. And in *As You Like It*, Arden has its own perils: harsh winds, cold, low wages, hard masters, dangerous creatures, weariness, hunting and death, hunger and exhaustion. The critic Jan Kott called it 'Bitter Arcadia', and characters in the play refer to it as 'a desert'.

- The 1937 production (opposite) presented the Forest of Arden as a painted backcloth (Rosalind holds a boar spear).

Shakespeare finds his story

As pages 176–7 show, the stories and plays of the pastoral romance tradition were very popular in Shakespeare's time. He used one of these stories, *Rosalynde, Euphues Golden Legacie*, by Thomas Lodge (1590) as the inspiration for the plot of *As You Like It*. He added the characters of Jaques, Touchstone, Audrey and William, but the following summary of *Rosalynde* (with the names of Shakespeare's characters in brackets) shows how closely he followed Lodge's tale:

- A nobleman dies, leaving three sons. The youngest son, Rosader (Orlando) is kept in poverty by the oldest son, Saladyne (Oliver).
- Saladyne plots that a wrestler kill Rosader. But Rosader defeats the wrestler. Rosalynde (Rosalind) watches the fight and falls in love with Rosader. She is the daughter of the rightful king who has been overthrown and now lives in exile.
- Saladyne again plots to kill Rosader, who flees to the Forest of Arden together with his loyal servant Adam Spencer (Adam). He and Adam receive hospitality from the exiled king.
- Rosalynde is banished from court. She flees with Alinda (Celia), daughter of the wrongful king, to the Forest of Arden. They disguise themselves as Ganymede and Aliena.
- They overhear a young shepherd (Silvius) telling an old shepherd (Corin) of his unrequited love for Phoebe (Phebe), a shepherdess. They give money to the shepherds.
- Rosader writes love poems to Rosalynde, who, as Ganymede, encourages Rosader to woo her as if she were Rosalynde. Aliena conducts a mock wedding of Rosalynde and Rosader. Phoebe falls in love with Ganymede.
- Rosader rescues his brother from a lion. Saladyne and Aliena fall in love. Rosalynde drops her disguise as Ganymede.
- Three marriages are celebrated.

• Step into role as Shakespeare. How do you defend yourself against the accusation of plagiarism (stealing other people's ideas and writing)?

Shakespeare also added songs to his dramatic re-working of Thomas Lodge's tale. Here Amiens sings to the exiled court.

The pastoral romance tradition

As Shakespeare wrote *As You Like It*, he was much influenced by what is now called the pastoral romance tradition. It was (and still is) made up of two major strands: 'pastoral' and 'romance'.

Pastoral

Pastoral was a literature and drama that idealised nature and rural life. It presented the country as far superior to the city, a place of escape. The country taught moral lessons ('books in the running brooks,/Sermons in stones, and good in everything'). In the country, remote from the town, human nature could be changed for good.

The pastoral tradition has a history that stretches back over 2,000 years to the Greek poet Theocritus (310–250 BC). He and other writers of classical antiquity created a golden world of peaceful and harmonious country life. This rural idyll was peopled by beautiful shepherdesses and shepherds ('pastor' in Latin means shepherd). They were poets, philosophers and lovers (and were often aristocrats in disguise as humble country folk).

Shakespeare would certainly have heard the pastoral tradition in folk tales such as that of Robin Hood and his Merry Men in Sherwood Forest. He would also have read some of its most famous literary expressions, written in his own lifetime. These included Sir Philip Sidney's *Arcadia* (1590), and Edmund Spenser's *The Shepheardes Calendar* (1579) and *The Faerie Queene* (1590/6).

Romance

The romance tradition largely derives from stories of love and chivalry which were very popular in the Middle Ages, for example, tales of King Arthur, the *Song of Roland*, *Roman de la Rose* and Chaucer's *Knight's Tale*. It dealt with the trials of young knights, and presented two views of love: courtly and romantic.

'Courtly love' was sexless and idealised. It put women 'on a pedestal' and worshipped them as unattainable goddesses. Only by long devotion, many trials and much suffering, could a man win his ideal woman, the 'fair, cruel maid' of literature. 'Romantic love' was also idealised and unsexual, but it included 'love at first sight'. Marriage was seen as its natural result.

Pastoral romance

The two earlier traditions increasingly merged into pastoral romance. Indeed, Sidney's and Spenser's work mentioned above as 'pastoral' can equally be thought of as 'romance'. Pastoral romance literature thus often included certain major features:

- *Shepherds*: lovesick shepherds, scornful shepherdesses.
- *Forests*: where magical transformations occur, and true love flourishes after rigorous testing; a place of deposed rulers, 'merry men', kindly outlaws and magicians.
- *Journeys*: a young knight leaves court to travel and seek his fortune;
- *Adventures*: he has many adventures in remote places;
- *Adversity*: he is beset by misfortune and undergoes many trials from which he learns;
- *Love*: he loves a beautiful woman. She occupies all his thoughts.
- *Faithfulness*: constancy (fidelity) is highly valued.
- *Coincidence*: all kinds of improbabilities and coincidences occur.
- *Fathers*: a beautiful woman has a harsh father.
- *Disguise*: mistaken identity and disguise feature in many stories.
- *Happy endings*: the knight marries his beloved, and the stories end with forgiveness, reconciliations and virtue triumphant.

Many members of Shakespeare's audience came to the Globe Theatre with a deep knowledge of pastoral romance literature. They expected to see its themes, characters and conventions portrayed on stage. Shakespeare fulfilled their expectations, but he also gave his audience something radically different. *As You Like It* shows that women can more than hold their own in the battle of the sexes. Rosalind takes the lead, directing and controlling the process of wooing – and falling head over heels in love herself.

- Work through the list above and identify how each element is represented in *As You Like It*.

- Talk together about how the pastoral and romance traditions live on today. For example, are films like *Titanic* and *Shakespeare in Love* romances? Which advertisements use 'pastoral' (countryside images) to sell their products?

The language of *As You Like It*

1 Verse and prose – 'Didst thou hear these verses?'

Over half of *As You Like It* is in prose: almost 1300 lines against just over 1100 lines of verse. How did Shakespeare decide whether to write in verse or prose? In his time, the play-writing convention was that high-status characters spoke in verse, and that prose was used for comedy or by low-status characters.

But Shakespeare never followed any convention slavishly. Rosalind and Celia are high-status characters (they are both princesses), yet much of their language is in prose. Silvius and Phebe, the shepherd and shepherdess (low status), speak in verse. It may be that as he wrote *As You Like It*, Shakespeare used prose or verse depending on whether he felt the situation to be 'comic' or 'serious'. But even that explanation is questionable: Oliver uses prose as he urges Charles the wrestler to harm Orlando (a 'serious' episode).

a Check through the play to discover which characters speak only in verse or in prose. Then select one Act and work through it identifying where prose switches to verse, or verse to prose. Give explanations for your findings.

b Most of the verse in the play is blank verse (unrhymed). Each ten-syllable line has five alternating unstressed (x) and stressed (/) syllables (iambic pentameter), as when Rosalind describes her height:

x / x / x / x / x /
Because that I am more than common tall

To experience the rhythm of iambic pentameter, read a few lines aloud from any of the verse speeches in the play. Pronounce each syllable very clearly as if it were a separate word. As you speak, beat out the five-beat rhythm (clap your hands or tap your desk).

c The songs, Orlando's poems, Phebe's letter and Hymen's blessings are all in verse, but not in the five-beat rhythm of iambic pentameter. Speak aloud a few lines of each to discover their distinctive rhythms.

d Invent a few blank verse lines describing your response to the play.

2 Imagery – 'Men are April when they woo …'

Imagery is the use of emotionally charged words and phrases which conjure up vivid mental pictures in the imagination. Such images intensify the dramatic and emotional impact of the play and help to create its distinctive atmosphere and themes. But in *As You Like It*, Shakespeare also gently mocks the use of imagery. In Act 3 Scene 6, lines 8–27, he gives Phebe twenty lines in which she ridicules the image that a lover's eyes can wound.

All Shakespeare's imagery uses metaphor or simile. A simile compares one thing to another using 'like' ('creeping like snail unwillingly to school') or 'as' ('my age is as a lusty winter'). A metaphor is also a comparison. It does not use 'like' or 'as' but suggests that two dissimilar things are actually the same. Examples are Rosalind labelling Silvius 'a tame snake', Orlando calling himself 'a rotten tree', and Touchstone insulting Corin as 'worms' meat'.

Personification is a particular type of imagery. It turns things or ideas into human persons ('the good housewife Fortune'), giving them human feelings or body parts ('the swift foot of Time'). Jaques and Orlando use personification to bid each other a mocking farewell as 'Signor Love' and 'Monsieur Melancholy'.

As You Like It contains a wide range of imagery, particularly that of animals, country life, hunting and theatre ('All the world's a stage'). On every page of the play you will find at least one example of imagery, and often many more. Turn to two or three pages at random. Identify the images on each page and suggest how they add to the dramatic appeal of the scene, for example, in creating atmosphere or conveying a sense of character or theme.

3 Lists – 'I will name you the degrees'

One of Shakespeare's favourite methods with language was to accumulate words or phrases rather like a list. He knew that 'piling up' item on item, incident on incident, can intensify description, atmosphere, character and dramatic effect. The most famous example is Jaques' 'seven ages of man' speech, and there are many other lists in the play. A few of the longer ones are: Corin's list of his contentments (Act 3 Scene 3, lines 53–6), Rosalind's breathless list of questions about Orlando 'What did he …?' (Act 3 Scene 3, lines 185–8), her ten 'marks' of a man in love 'A lean cheek …' (Act 3 Scene 3, lines 312–18), the eighteen ways in which she 'cured' a lover (Act 3 Scene 3, lines 336–46), Jaques' description of different kinds of melancholy (Act 4 Scene 1, lines 9–16), Silvius' list of what it is to love (Act 5 Scene 2, lines 67–82) and Touchstone's twice repeated catalogue of how to avoid a duel (Act 5 Scene 4, lines 62–83).

Choose one of the lists from the paragraph above (or one of your own choice from elsewhere in the play). Speak it in a style you think suitable, then work with others to act out the list in some way.

4 Songs – 'Come, warble, come'

There are seven songs in the play: 'Under the greenwood tree' and Jaques' parody of it 'If it do come to pass' (Act 2 Scene 5), 'Blow, blow, thou winter wind' (Act 2 Scene 7), 'O sweet Oliver' (Act 3 Scene 4), 'What shall he have that killed the deer?' (Act 4 Scene 2), 'It was a lover and his lass' (Act 5 Scene 3) and 'Wedding is great Juno's crown' (Act 5 Scene 4).

The songs may be Shakespeare's response to the popularity of the children's acting companies of the time, whose singing attracted large audiences. Or perhaps there was a gifted singer in Shakespeare's own acting company, so Shakespeare inserted the songs specially for him. Or maybe Shakespeare thought the songs were particularly suited to the pastoral mood of the play. Whatever the explanation, Shakespeare wanted the audience to enjoy his songs, so select one and work out your own performance of it!

5 Repetition – 'O Phebe, Phebe, Phebe!'

Repeated words, phrases, rhythms and sounds add to the dramatic force of the play. Rhymes (repeated sounds) are most obvious in each of the songs, in Orlando's poems, in Phebe's letter and in the couplets which end some scenes. Some episodes have an almost ritualistic quality because particular phrases and rhythms are repeated, for example, Silvius' first appearance, with his refrain 'Thou hast not loved' (Act 2 Scene 4, lines 27–36); the echoing exchange between Orlando and Duke Senior 'If ever you have looked on better days' (Act 2 Scene 7, lines 113–26); the three lovers who repeat Silvius' litany of love 'And so am I for Phebe' (Act 5 Scene 2, lines 67–90); and Rosalind's promise to satisfy the wishes of each lover 'I will help you if I can' (Act 5 Scene 2, lines 92–100).

- Check the final two lines of each scene. How many of them are rhyming couplets? Suggest why Shakespeare chooses to end some scenes in this way.

6 Antithesis – 'To liberty, and not to banishment'

Although *As You Like It* is a comedy, it is full of conflict: brother versus brother, court versus country and the conflicts of love itself. Shakespeare's language powerfully conveys conflict through its use of antithesis: the opposition of words or phrases against each other, setting the word against the word.

Antithesis is most clearly seen in the verse sections of the play. For example, the first time verse is spoken, Duke Frederick says to Orlando 'The world esteemed thy father honourable/ But I did find him still mine enemy' (Act 1 Scene 2, lines 177–8). Here 'world' opposes 'I', and 'honourable' contrasts with 'enemy'. But the prose of the play also contains much antithesis, as in Celia's tart remark ('Was' is not 'is') to Rosalind's claim that she heard Orlando swear he was in love (Act 3 Scene 5, line 26). Choose a particular scene and work through it identifying how antithesis adds to dramatic tension.

7 Puns and wordplay – 'How now, wit, whither wander you?'

Shakespeare and his contemporaries loved wordplay of all kinds, and puns were especially popular. A pun is a play on words where the same sound or word has different meanings. Finding himself in the Forest of Arden, Touchstone puns on 'bear' and 'cross' and, in his tale of Jane Smile, and in his meeting with Jaques, on words which had sexual meanings for Elizabethans (Act 2 Scenes 4 and 7).

Rosalind puns on 'hart' (female deer) when, hearing that Orlando is dressed like a hunter, she cries 'He comes to kill my heart'. But the most intriguing wordplay comes when Rosalind (disguised as Ganymede) persuades Orlando to woo her/him. Take parts and speak the 'wooing scene' (Act 4 Scene 1, lines 31–176). Orlando thinks he is speaking to a boy, but Rosalind revels in the ambiguity that her disguise gives. She can speak as herself without Orlando knowing it. As you speak her language, pause at each personal pronoun (I, me, myself, and so on) and say just who she might have in mind.

Critics' forum

Early critics of *As You Like It* were much concerned with Rosalind and with the play as entertainment. Recent criticism has dealt with issues of gender, patriarchy, social hierarchy and personal identity. Use the following to explore your own responses to the play. Remember, you don't have to agree with any if you can justify your own interpretation.

By hastening to the end of his work, Shakespeare suppressed the dialogue between the usurper and the hermit, and lost an opportunity of exhibiting a moral lesson in which he might have found matter worthy of his highest powers. *Samuel Johnson, 1765*

It is the most ideal of any of (Shakespeare's) plays. It is a pastoral drama in which the interest arises more out of the sentiments and characters than out of the action or situation … Caprice and fancy reign and revel here, and stern necessity is banished to the court.
William Hazlitt, 1817

As You Like It is a criticism of the pastoral sentiment, an examination of certain familiar ideas concerning the simple life and the golden age … The result is something very curious. When Rosalind has made her last curtsy and the comedy is done, the pastoral sentiment is without a leg to stand on, and yet it stands; and not only stands but dances. The idea of the simple life has been smiled off the earth, and yet here it is, smiling back at us from every bough of Arden … The doctrine of the golden age has been as much created as destroyed.
Mark Van Doren, 1939

Shakespeare is not interested in a comforting pastoral dream. From the dark corridors of the duke's palace, the forest has all the inviting warmth of the escape world of the Golden Age. But those who make the journey find 'a desert inaccessible', where the wind bites shrewdly, and food is only to be had by hunting. Expecting a womb, they are faced with a challenge. The forest only helps those who help themselves.
David Jones, 1968

The play shows us not a court made simple, but a simple place made courtly. *A D Nuttall, 1972*

Behind Rosalind's disguise … lies the great Renaissance wish-dream of harmony between the masculine and feminine principles.
Anne Barton, 1973

[The play's] aristocratic protagonists formulate and enact an ideology: they express the particular interests of their own class as if these were identical with universal interests, with the interests of the whole society.
Elliot Krieger, 1979

Elizabeth's court by the end of the sixteenth century was increasingly adopting Duke Frederick's style of arbitrary and personalised decision-making. Profound questions were being asked about the legitimacy of the monarch's power, as well as about the new kind of thuggish profiteering personified by Orlando's older brother Oliver. Thus the many angry comments by Rosalind, Orlando, Adam and others about the 'fashion of these times', as well as Jaques' desire to 'cleanse the foul body of the infected world', must have held an extraordinary power over an audience caught up in a whirlwind of change, social disintegration and ultimately Civil War.
Stephen Unwin, 1994

With Orlando what you see is what you get. Rosalind on the other hand needs to be freed from the feminine role that projects so pale a version of the resourceful, noisy, energetic person she really is before she can love Orlando with all her might … when as Ganymede Rosalind sets out to cure Orlando of his inherited disease of courtly love, she is in earnest. He has no wish to be cured; it is she who needs to replace bad poetry and stereotyped reactions by true love and loyalty and these she draws from him in the person of a boy.
Germaine Greer, 1996

The forest people in *As You Like It* do not, actually, 'fleet the time carelessly'. They have hierarchy, property and money, and give little serious thought to living without them. Despite his sturdy independence, Orlando would rather subject himself to his brother's malice than take to the roads without money … luckily, he has Adam's savings and service, so he can travel in the style of a gentleman …. The outlaw band maintain, with scarcely a second thought, the hierarchy they observed at court. … (They) are not outside the state system; they are a government in waiting. The play presents a conflict within the ruling elite: which faction is to control the state and its resources?
Alan Sinfield, 1996

Staging *As You Like It*

Shakespeare probably wrote *As You Like It* around 1600, perhaps in response to the popularity of pastoral plays at that time. There is a tradition that this was the very first play acted at the Globe Theatre on London's Bankside and that Shakespeare played Adam in that production. Another tradition claims that *As You Like It* was performed before King James I in 1603. But no one knows for sure if these stories are true. There is no actual record of a performance during Shakespeare's lifetime.

The first historical record of a performance is of an adaptation in 1723, *Love in a Forest.* This cut out all the lower-class characters, substituted fencing with rapiers for the wrestling match and included lines, songs and characters from other Shakespeare plays. Jaques married Celia, and the mechanicals from *A Midsummer Night's Dream* performed their Pyramus and Thisbe play.

In 1740, the play was performed largely as Shakespeare had written it, and from then on it became one of the most popular and frequently performed of all his plays. In the eighteenth and nineteenth centuries, many leading actresses played Rosalind, and the success of a production was largely judged on who played the part.

In the last half of the nineteenth century, and early in the twentieth century, many productions attempted to put a very realistic Forest of Arden on stage (or what Victorians thought a forest was like). These included running streams, real trees, logs, grass, leaves and ferns. Some productions brought live animals on stage. Sheep and rabbits were common. One staging presented a whole herd of deer.

For many years at Stratford-upon-Avon, productions of *As You Like It* included a stuffed deer from nearby Charlecote Park (where Shakespeare was supposed to have poached deer, and fled to London to escape the wrath of the landowner). In 1919, the director of that year's production refused to include the stuffed deer. Many local people were outraged at the break with tradition. The director was insulted in the street.

Staging the Forest of Arden at London's National Theatre.

By the second half of the twentieth century, the earlier emphasis on the play as mainly a starring vehicle for the actress playing Rosalind had given way to 'company productions' in which all the actors contributed significantly to the success of each performance. Gender issues also became more central, for example, in several all-male modern dress productions. Just as in Shakespeare's time, all female parts were played by males (see page 169).

Social issues have also been more prominently stressed in modern productions, in the emphasis on the harsh political realities of Duke

Frederick's court and the exploitation of the natural world by the exiled court. The 1978 BBC production was shot in the grounds of Glamis Castle in Scotland, but a 1992 film set Arden in a modern urban wasteland.

As You Like It is also popular outside England. In Italy, Salvador Dali designed surrealist sets for a production in Rome. Before the unification of Germany, a famous 1977 production in Berlin implied that the Forest of Arden (a 'free' place) was like West Berlin surrounded by the socialist German Democratic Republic. The production included appearances of Robin Hood and Robinson Crusoe.

Five directors

Work in groups of five. You are each a director who wants to put on a production of *As You Like It*. But you have very different conceptions of the play! Step into role and argue why 'your' version is the most appropriate.

1 *'It's about nature.'* You believe that the play is about the goodness of the natural world: how the forest, real animals, and so on provide moral guidance for human beings. You want to stage the play outdoors, in a real forest.

2 *'It's about art and artifice.'* You believe that the play is about art and illusion: that Shakespeare is mocking the pastoral tradition in literature and drama (see page 176). You want to stage the play in a procenium arch theatre using modern technology.

3 *'It's about social criticism.'* You believe that the play is Shakespeare's response to the rebellious protests against land enclosures and food shortages of Elizabethan England. You want to stage the play in a disused factory building.

4 *'It's about gender.'* You believe that the play uses cross-dressing to explore issues of gender and patriarchy. You want to perform the play with either an all-male, or an all-female cast.

5 *'It's only a play.'* You believe that the play is simply an entertainment to make people happy, and that it has no 'message' or critical intent.

'True delights.' Hymen presides over the revelries at the end of the play in this Royal Shakespeare Company production.

William Shakespeare 1564–1616

1564 Born Stratford-upon-Avon, eldest son of John and Mary Shakespeare.
1582 Marries Anne Hathaway of Shottery, near Stratford.
1583 Daughter, Susanna, born.
1585 Twins, son and daughter, Hamnet and Judith, born.
1592 First mention of Shakespeare in London. Robert Greene, another playwright, described Shakespeare as 'an upstart crow beautified with our feathers ...'. Greene seems to have been jealous of Shakespeare. He mocked Shakespeare's name, calling him 'the only Shake-scene in a country' (presumably because Shakespeare was writing successful plays).
1595 A shareholder in 'The Lord Chamberlain's Men', an acting company that became extremely popular.
1596 Son Hamnet dies, aged eleven.
Father, John, granted arms (acknowledged as a gentleman).
1597 Buys New Place, the grandest house in Stratford.
1598 Acts in Ben Jonson's *Every Man in His Humour*.
1599 Globe Theatre opens on Bankside. Performances in the open air.
1601 Father, John, dies.
1603 James I grants Shakespeare's company a royal patent: 'The Lord Chamberlain's Men' became 'The King's Men' and played about twelve performances each year at court.
1607 Daughter, Susanna, marries Dr John Hall.
1608 Mother, Mary, dies.
1609 'The King's Men' begin performing indoors at Blackfriars Theatre.
1610 Probably returned from London to live in Stratford.
1616 Daughter, Judith, marries Thomas Quiney.
Dies. Buried in Holy Trinity Church, Stratford-upon-Avon.

The plays and poems

(no one knows exactly when he wrote each play)

1589–1595 *The Two Gentlemen of Verona*, *The Taming of the Shrew*, *First*, *Second and Third Parts of King Henry VI*, *Titus Andronicus*, *King Richard III*, *The Comedy of Errors*, *Love's Labour's Lost*, *A Midsummer Night's Dream*, *Romeo and Juliet*, *King Richard II* (and the long poems *Venus and Adonis* and *The Rape of Lucrece*).

1596–1599 *King John*, *The Merchant of Venice*, *First and Second Parts of King Henry IV*, *The Merry Wives of Windsor*, *Much Ado About Nothing*, *King Henry V*, *Julius Caesar* (and probably the *Sonnets*).

1600–1605 *As You Like It*, *Hamlet*, *Twelfth Night*, *Troilus and Cressida*, *Measure for Measure*, *Othello*, *All's Well That Ends Well*, *Timon of Athens*, *King Lear*.

1606–1611 *Macbeth*, *Antony and Cleopatra*, *Pericles*, *Coriolanus*, *The Winter's Tale*, *Cymbeline*, *The Tempest*.

1613 *King Henry VIII*, *The Two Noble Kinsmen* (both probably with John Fletcher).

1623 Shakespeare's plays published as a collection (now called the First Folio).